W9-CAV-091

THE TEN OFFENSES

THE
TEN
OFFENSES

PAT
ROBERTSON

INTEGRITY®

P U B L I S H E R S

Nashville

THE TEN OFFENSES

Copyright © 2004 by Pat Robertson.

Published by Integrity Publishers, a division of Integrity Media, Inc., 5250 Virginia Way, Suite 110, Brentwood, TN 37027.

HELPING PEOPLE WORLDWIDE EXPERIENCE *the* MANIFEST PRESENCE *of* GOD.

All rights reserved. No portion of this book may be reproduced, stored in a retrieval system, or transmitted in any form or by any means—electronic, mechanical, photocopy, recording, or any other—except for brief quotations in printed reviews, without the prior written permission of the publisher.

Unless otherwise indicated, Scripture quotations are taken from The Holy Bible, New International Version, copyright © 1973, 1978, 1984, International Bible Society. Used by permission of Zondervan Bible Publishers.

Scripture quotations marked KJV are taken from the King James Version of the Bible. Scripture quotations marked NLT are taken from The Holy Bible, New Living Translation, copyright © 1996. Used by permission of Tyndale House Publishers, Inc., Wheaton, Illinois. All rights reserved.

ISBN 1-59145-126-4

Printed in the United States of America
04 05 06 07 08 BVG 9 8 7 6 5 4 3 2 1

CONTENTS

Now all has been heard;
Here is the conclusion of the matter:
Fear God and keep his commandments,
for this is the whole duty of man.
For God will bring every deed into judgment,
including every hidden thing,
whether it is good or evil.

—ECCLESIASTES 12:13–14

PROLOGUE

Of all the dispositions and habits which lead to political prosperity, religion and morality are indispensable supports. In vain would that man claim tribute of patriotism, who should labor to subvert these great pillars of human happiness.

— PRESIDENT GEORGE WASHINGTON
in his farewell address (1796)

THE UNITED STATES OF AMERICA is by every measure the richest, most powerful, most charitable, and most blessed nation that has ever existed in the history of the world. The empires of Babylon, Persia, Greece, and Rome pale in significance when compared to the United States. We must exercise great care that we do not destroy the foundations that have made us what we are.

Importantly, this nation has become a beacon of hope for people from all over the world. Our Christian culture has opened its arms to Jews from Eastern Europe, Muslims from the Middle East, Hindus from India, and immigrants from Europe, Latin America, Asia, and the islands of the seas. This magnificent land offers everyone who comes here freedom and opportunity to achieve great success in science, medicine, education, business, government, the arts, and much more.

As we will see in the chapters that follow, history shows that those who founded the United States consciously intended America to be a Christian nation, guided above all else by the truths of the Bible. The fundamental principles for the laws and liberties of this new nation were found in the Ten Commandments of the Old Testament and the Sermon on the Mount of the New Testament.

Revisionist historians have tried to blur the facts of history, but the documented evidence of our origins is too powerful to suppress. It was a Christian America that opened its arms to the world and guaranteed what we now pledge as "liberty and justice for all." It was the spiritual, moral, and ethical teaching of Christianity that brought about our unparalleled prosperity as a nation.

From 1607, when the first English-speaking settlers planted a cross on the shores of the Atlantic Ocean in Virginia, until the days following World War II, the American people assented to two foundational principles: first, that the God of the Bible exists and we are one nation under Him; and second, that the Holy Bible is the ultimate guide for our nation and for our lives. During this time, Americans readily affirmed the words of George Washington, our first president, who said in his farewell address, "Of all the dispositions and habits which lead to political prosperity, religion and morality are indispensable supports. In vain would that man claim tribute of patriotism, who should labor to subvert these great pillars of human happiness." We believed the sentiments of Daniel Webster, who said, "If we abide by the principles taught in the Bible, our nation will go on prospering." And we said a hearty amen to the words of French philosopher Alexis de Tocqueville, who wrote of the primary role of religion in American life.

THE TYRANNY OF ESTABLISHED RELIGION

I was born during the Depression in a small Virginia university town. My father spent his entire life in public service. He went to the United States Senate in 1956 to fill the term of the late Senator Carter Glass. He, along with men like Richard Russell, Harry Byrd, John Stennis, Sam Irwin, and Lyndon Johnson, made up the group of senior southern Democrats who, as committee chairmen, played a dominant role in the United States Senate. My early life was steeped in Virginia politics and the philosophies of men such as Thomas Jefferson, George Washington, Patrick Henry, Robert E. Lee, and Stonewall Jackson.

My family was Baptist, and I learned from my father the accounts of the jailings, the beatings, and the exorbitant fines that the established Anglican Church in Virginia exacted on my Baptist ancestors. Baptists were taxed to support Anglican clergy and fined if they did not attend Anglican Sunday services. They were fined if they attempted marriage outside the Anglican Church. They were jailed and whipped if they preached the gospel of Jesus Christ. Virginia Baptists urged James Madison to present Jefferson's "Statute for Religious Freedom" to the Virginia legislature. Without a doubt, my father and I understood what James Madison was thinking when he wrote the First Amendment to the United States Constitution, forbidding an "establishment of religion." Thomas Jefferson, James Madison, and my ancestors in Virginia had experienced the tyranny of an established religion, and they did not like it.

An established church was one thing, but belief in God and the Bible was entirely different. In fact, the founders considered belief in God a vital thing. They were convinced that the Ten Commandments were basic to all our laws and public morality. Never would my father and his contemporaries have imagined that Jefferson, Madison, or Washington thought the acknowledgment of a Supreme Being constituted an "establishment of religion."

ERODING AMERICA'S SPIRITUAL FOUNDATION

For decades, certain "elites" in America have been hard at work to banish the God of the Bible from all discussion and debate concerning our most important national issues—issues that are, in fact, matters of life and death. Because this war between the spiritual and secular vision for America is long and slow, and the battles are fought in distant courtrooms, most Americans are only vaguely aware of the alarmingly serious threat to our nation's foundation and Christian heritage. We have failed to recognize the relentless, ongoing war for America's soul.

Never would any of us have dreamed that one day in 1980 the Supreme Court would deny to schoolchildren across America the privilege of learning God's basic principles of human conduct found in the Ten Commandments. And who could have imagined that in August of 2003 a U.S. district court judge would order a monument inscribed with the Ten Commandments to be removed from the Alabama Supreme Court building's central rotunda?

Most Americans embrace these commandments as an indispensable part of our nation's moral heritage. Consider this. The Commandments are on the floor of the National Archives building. A bronze statue of Moses is in the Library of Congress. In the Supreme Court, Moses stands at the center on the east portico, as well as on a frieze inside the courtroom. The Ten Commandments are carved on the wooden doors leading to the Supreme Court. The marble relief of the face of Moses is placed directly opposite the Speaker's chair in the House of Representatives. In the Capitol Rotunda is a depiction of the sister ship of the *Mayflower,* the *Speedwell,* where the Bible is open on the chaplain's lap and the pilgrim motto "In God we trust, God with us" is plainly visible on the ship's sails.

In my anger, I join the majority of people across this land who protest the removal of the Ten Commandments from the public square. Opinion polls clearly show that the majority of the American people want children to pray in school, want to say the Pledge of Allegiance (which includes the words "one nation under God"), and want to allow the display of the Ten Commandments, as was intended by our founders.

The incident in Alabama is just one small piece of the greater erosion of Judeo-Christian morality that is occurring all around us. As those who oppose God's standards continue to win ground in both courts and culture, none of us is safe from the devastating consequences. And what we are about to see, if we do not stand against the erosion of our spiritual foundation, is a virtual earthquake of violence, immorality, and untold suffering.

If that were not bad enough, also at stake is nothing less than our personal freedom. The fundamental freedom recognized in democracies is the right of the people to govern themselves. If that right is taken away by agenda-driven judges bent on emasculating the duly elected Congress and state legislatures, freedom will be transferred from the majority to an elite, secular minority—a new class that will be more authoritarian than any of us can imagine.

Many Americans in education, law, medicine, psychology, the arts, and the media seem to have an agenda to erase God and biblical morality from our nation. Why are they offended by the Ten Commandments? The answer is painfully obvious: They perceive any system of moral absolutes that defines or restrains their choices as antiquated and oppressive, dangerously limiting their rights. Simply put, the Ten Commandments represent absolute truth, and that cramps their style. But to those who understand their deeper meaning, the Ten Commandments are unbelievable blessings that provide safety, security, peace of mind, and a life free from many troubles.

During the past two hundred years, oppressed Hindus, Buddhists, Muslims, and Jews have flooded into America because our Christian culture respects their individual liberties and offers endless opportunities, just as our founders intended. What other culture in the world shows such respect for each individual's rights? Why allow liberal court justices, unthinking legislatures, and fiercely secular organizations to destroy our nation's greatest and most compelling fundamental treasure—our spiritual foundation? Pluralism thrives in America as a result of our Christian heritage, not in spite of it.

THE PURPOSE OF THE TEN OFFENSES

My purpose in this book is to provide a healthy understanding of what the Ten Commandments mean, why they are an offense to some, and how obedience to them can bless our lives and our country. The first chapter reveals startling facts about the founding of this nation. Chapter 2 details appalling evidence drawn from actual cases that show the unchecked power grab by the Supreme Court and the unwillingness of Congress to use its constitutional privileges to restrain the Court. Chapter 3 details the vendetta of the Court and its allies against the Ten Commandments. In chapters 4 through 13, the Ten Commandments—and our nation's observance of them—are held up to scrutiny. And the appendix clearly shows the spiritual foundation upon which all fifty state governments were established.

It is time for America to return to its spiritual foundation. God gave us the Ten Commandments as a rich source of blessing for our nation and for every citizen, regardless of his or her religious heritage. God's laws do not issue from the heart of an oppressor. They come from a loving Father, and they are meant for our good and our protection.

We must stand strong. I have come to the conclusion that if we are to check the rapid erosion of our society, we who believe in the God of the Bible must insist that the Ten Commandments be honored in the public square. It's my prayer that a deeper understanding of each commandment will draw you closer to God so that your life will be enriched and abundantly blessed.

ONE

Founding a Christian Nation

We, . . . Having undertaken for the Glory of God, and Advancement of the Christian Faith, and the Honor of our King and Country, a voyage to plant the first colony in the northern parts of Virginia; do . . . solemnly and mutually in the Presence of God and one another, covenant and combine ourselves together into a civil Body Politick . . .

—MAYFLOWER COMPACT (1620)

IT WAS A SLIGHTLY CHILLY APRIL DAY in the year 1607 when three tiny boats, scarcely bigger than twenty-first-century cabin cruisers, appeared on the horizon of the Atlantic Ocean and sailed toward the coastline of North America, where they dropped anchor in deep water just offshore. One hundred twenty bone-weary English travelers then took their turns climbing down into long boats that deposited them onto the sandy beach.

After an agonizingly long journey during which the travelers had been packed into their tiny vessels, they were intoxicated with the feel of land under their feet and the scent of woods and flowers. They scrambled up the adjoining sand dunes in search of wild berries, fresh water, and firewood. The next three days were spent in exploration and profuse apologies to one another for the contemptible attitudes many had displayed during their most trying voyage. But they had come to settle a continent, not to beachcomb on this point of land they named Cape Henry, after Henry, the son of King James I of England.

On April 29, 1607, their spiritual leader, Reverend Robert Hunt, suggested they memorialize their landing in this New World. He directed that the seven-foot oak cross they had brought from England be carried from one of the ships and planted firmly in the sand of what years later became the city of Virginia Beach, Virginia. These brave pioneer men and women then knelt in prayer around the rough-hewn cross and claimed this new land for the glory of God and His Son, Jesus Christ.

Centuries later, in the 1930s, an official monument was erected at this site (although, regrettably, it is no longer there) with a stone cross and the following inscription:

> *Act One, Scene One of the unfolding drama that became the United States of America.*

Having begun this new land with a prayer meeting, these first permanent English settlers to America reboarded their boats and sailed up a large river that they named the James. In a protected harbor on the northeast bank some fifteen miles upstream, they founded a settlement called Jamestown, so named in honor of their king, James of England.

The central and largest building constructed for the tiny settlement was a church where all of the settlers worshiped God, observed the sacraments of their Christian faith, and were taught to obey the commandments of God. The concept of "separation of church and state" would have been unthinkable to them because their Christian faith and their civic government were as one. Their concepts of life, freedom, and ordered liberty were framed principally by the Ten Commandments of the Old Testament and the Sermon on the Mount of the New Testament.

Without dispute, the United States of America began as a nation of Christians and as a Christian nation framed by the commandments of God.

THE MAYFLOWER COMPACT

Thirteen years later, another band of English settlers sailed on a boat called the *Mayflower* and reached Cape Cod on the Atlantic coastline of what later became the state of Massachusetts. After coming ashore in November of 1620, they drafted a foundational document known as the Mayflower Compact, which historians tell us was the first formal document for self-government drafted in America. Here is what it said (emphases added):

> *In the name of God,* Amen. We, whose names are under-written, the Loyal Subjects of our dread Sovereign Lord, King James, *by the Grace of God,* of England, France and Ireland, King, Defender of the Faith, . . . Having undertaken for the *Glory of God, and Advancement of the Christian Faith,* and the Honor of our King and Country, a voyage to plant the first colony in the northern parts of Virginia; do by these presents, solemnly and mutually *in the Presence of God* and one another, covenant and combine ourselves together into a civil Body Politick, for our better Ordering and Preservation, and Furtherance of the Ends aforesaid; and by Virtue hereof to enact, constitute, and frame, such just and equal Laws, Ordinances, Acts, Constitutions and Offices, from time to time, as shall be thought most meet and convenient for the General good of the Colony; unto which we promise all due submission and obedience. In Witness whereof we have hereunto subscribed our names at Cape Cod the eleventh of November, in the Reign of our Sovereign Lord, King James of England, France and Ireland, the eighteenth, and of Scotland the fifty-fourth. *Anno Domini,* 1620.

Again, contemporary political correctness and revisionist history notwithstanding, the founders of the United States of America did so to "advance the Christian faith and bring glory to God." Some today may not like that fact, but it is true nonetheless.

It would have been unthinkable that the teaching of the Holy Bible, which laid out the concepts of Christianity and, in turn, the views of "just and equal laws, ordinances, acts, constitutions, and offices," would be denied to children in their schools or stripped from the public square by court orders in subsequent years.

THE CHARTER OF MASSACHUSETTS BAY

To underscore their clear intentions, these *Mayflower* settlers, and those who came later, set forth the full scope of their concept of government—including a governor, legislature, and various courts —in what was called the Charter of Massachusetts Bay. In this charter, they included these words, " . . . whereby our said people, inhabitants there, may be so religiously, peaceably, and civilly governed, as their good life and orderly conversation may win and incite the natives of country, to *the knowledge and obedience of the only true God and Savior of mankind and the Christian faith*" (emphasis added).

This new nation was not polytheistic, multicultural, Islamic, Hindu, Buddhist, animist, or atheistic. It was a Christian nation intended to be governed by religious people who were guided by the precepts of the Holy Bible.

In 1663, the Charter for Rhode Island and Providence described their founders as people who were "pursuing with peaceable and loyal minds, their sober, serious and religious intentions, *of godly edifying themselves, and one another, in the holy Christian faith and worship as they were persuaded*" (emphasis added).

Written ninety-four years after the founding of Jamestown, the Delaware Charter of 1701 expressly states: "Almighty God being the only Lord of Conscience, Father of Lights and Spirits; and the Author as well as object of all divine Knowledge, Faith, and Worship, who only doth enlighten the Minds, and persuade and convenience the Understandings of People . . . *And that all persons who also profess to believe in Jesus Christ, the Savior of the world, shall be capable . . . to serve this government in any capacity, both legislatively and executively . . .* " (emphasis added).

THIRTEEN COLONIES BASED ON FAITH

From 1607 until 1776, thirteen colonies came into being in this new land. By 1776, there were an estimated three million inhabitants of the thirteen colonial states, of which some 2,500 were Jewish (according to the World Jewish Congress), a handful were atheists and agnostics, and the remainder were primarily Protestant Christians.

Although the colonies' leaders had studied the writings of contemporary European philosophers as well as the sages of Greece and Rome, their concepts of ordered liberty, the dignity of the individual, the proper role of government, and true private and public morality came from the Bible. The great thinkers of the Reformation, especially John Calvin and Martin Luther, and expository sermons preached by gifted men of God throughout the land, were also pivotal to their thinking. Without an understanding of the Bible, especially the Ten Commandments of Moses the great lawgiver, it is impossible to understand the constitutions, the laws, and the customs of either colonial or modern America.

Some 169 years after the founding of Jamestown, the new nation was confronted with an intolerable situation. King George III of England, who was an autocratic tyrant, and the British Parliament, which was led by Lord North, considered the American colonies not as a prized part of the British Empire but as a cash cow to be repeatedly milked of its wealth to support the government of England.

The colonists were taxed on the importations of silk, linen, manufactured goods, gunpowder, and tea, as well as the exportation of tobacco and other agricultural products. To add further indignity, the colonists were required to quarter British troops in their homes and to pay taxes to support them. Although each colony had its own legislature, those legislative bodies had little voice in setting taxes. The British Parliament set taxes on the colonies and then ratcheted them up with studied indifference to the suffering they caused. Frequent colonial petitions were rebuffed or ignored by the government in London. So seething discontent began to bubble over into talk of rebellion. The abuses were clear, and the rallying cry of the colonists was equally clear: "Taxation without representation is tyranny."

THE DECLARATION OF INDEPENDENCE

An assembly of distinguished representatives from each of the thirteen American colonies assembled in Philadelphia in the summer of 1776 to catalogue their grievances and to submit a declaration setting forth the reasons that the thirteen English colonies in America should become a separate nation, independent from their mother country, England.

The vast majority of these representatives were Christians! All had been taught the Bible. In their declaration, they spoke of truths that were "self-evident." The first "self-evident truth" was that all men are *created* equal. They all assumed the biblical concept of creation.

They understood that God had created a world order in which all people, regardless of race or religious heritage, held the right to "life, liberty, and the pursuit of happiness." And what is the "pursuit of happiness?" It is none other than personal fulfillment by each individual, without hindrance by government, of the purposes for which he or she has been created. I can only presume that those who drafted the Declaration of Independence were familiar with God's words to the prophet Jeremiah: "Before I formed you in the womb I knew you, . . . I appointed you as a prophet to the nations"

(Jeremiah 1:5). Finding that ordained purpose, just as Jeremiah did, will indeed bring happiness and is man's highest goal.

Historians believe that John Adams, our second president, who was a dedicated Christian and learned Bible scholar, formulated the essential concepts of the Declaration. Adams recommended that Thomas Jefferson of Virginia, a man highly regarded for the felicity of his writing, draft the language of the document.

FAITH AT THE CENTER OF INDEPENDENCE

And so it was that on July 4, 1776, my collateral ancestor, Benjamin Harrison, was the presiding officer when the delegates pledged their lives to the cause of freedom and signed the Declaration of Independence for what was to become the United States of America. At our independence, our rallying cry as a nation sprang from the firm conviction that we should fight for the liberty that had been given to each one of us by our Creator—God. In the twenty-first century, we would do well to remember that the essential support of our liberty is our faith in God. Strip away the affirmation of faith in God from the public arena, and the only support of liberty standing against the armed might of cruel tyrants is the fickle passion of public opinion.

The Declaration of Independence sets forth in clear but peaceable language the abuses inflicted by England on its colonies in North America and the reasons that the colonists deemed it necessary to sever the formal ties with their mother country. The British government could have acceded to the colonists' request, granted them independence, and entered into a treaty of friendship, comity, and beneficial trade with the colonies. Instead, the British regarded the Declaration of Independence as an act of rebellion to be crushed by force of arms. Each hostile act of the British thereafter merely served to harden the colonists' resolve.

Eloquent Virginia statesman Patrick Henry echoed the prevailing sentiment of his fellow countrymen when he thundered forth: "Is life so dear or peace so sweet as to be purchased at the price of chains and slavery? Forbid it, Almighty God! I know not what others may do, but as for me, give me liberty or give me death."

Many died in the cause of freedom. The suffering of the American colonists and their soldiers on the battlefield was intense.

COLONISTS PRAY FOR GOD'S PROTECTION

Yet on two notable instances, what seemed like miracles saved the colonial armies from annihilation. Here are the stories of what actually happened.

General George Washington's men had fought valiantly to prevent a British takeover of New York. Despite their heroism, the American forces had been pushed to the water's edge in Brooklyn at the western tip of Long Island. By nightfall, the British had moved into position to annihilate the Americans the following morning. But during the night, a dense fog moved into the area. By morning, the fog completely shielded Washington's forces from British sight. Slowly but surely, every man, every artillery piece, and every horse was quietly loaded on boats and barges and ferried across the Hudson River to the safety of New Jersey, where the Americans could resupply and fight on. Later that morning, when the fog lifted and the British sprung the trap they had so carefully put in place, they found not one single American remaining. All had escaped because of what the American forces believed was a direct miracle of God.

Later in the war, a second miraculous event occurred. Lord Cornwallis of England had taken a position on the riverbank in Yorktown, Virginia. The sea lanes at the mouth of the river were blockaded by a French fleet that had arrived to help the Americans. Cornwallis was surrounded, but he knew aid was coming to him by way of a large British force from the south. Again, as was the case on

Long Island, a dense fog settled over the river at Yorktown, making maneuvers by the British ships impossible. Cornwallis realized that without reinforcements, his situation was untenable. Facing a crushing defeat, he did the wise thing and surrendered his army to Washington, ending what we know as the Revolutionary War.

The colonists had offered fervent prayers to God. And, despite all human reason to the contrary, they believed God had sustained them, blessed them, and miraculously delivered them, helping them to defeat the armies of the most powerful nation on earth.

GOD IN THE CONSTITUTION

Eleven years after the signing of the Declaration of Independence, delegates from the thirteen states met again in Philadelphia to craft a constitution for "a more perfect union" than they had known under the loose Articles of Confederation, which had been their governing charter following the Revolutionary War.

The Constitution for the emerging United States of America was signed by George Washington on September 17, "in the year of our Lord" 1787. To those who say that there is no mention of God or Jesus Christ in the Constitution, I ask this question: Which "Lord" was Washington referring to? Lord North? King George, Lord of England? Or was it the Lord Jesus Christ, who was born 1,787 years previously and whose birth became the point of reference for all Western calendars—those events "Before Christ" (BC) and those events *"Anno Domini"* (AD), the year of our Lord?

Having signed "in the year of our Lord," Washington was faced with no protest, no minority report, and no claim that the rights of non-Christians were being violated. When he affirmed in the Constitution that Jesus Christ was Lord of the assembled delegates, and in fact of the entire nation, no dissent was forthcoming because this statement was a fact not in dispute at the time of the signing of the Constitution of the United States.

The Constitution drafted by the Constitutional Convention in 1787 could not become effective unless ratified by at least three-fourths of the states. The states wanted a strong, effective central government, but they insisted on a bill of rights that would prevent the proposed national legislature from trampling individual liberties or the clear prerogatives of the states.

"CONGRESS SHALL MAKE NO LAW . . ."

James Madison of Virginia—who studied theology at Princeton University under the great minister statesman John Witherspoon—along with fellow Virginian George Mason, was asked to draft ten amendments to the Constitution in a fashion not unlike the Ten Commandments of Moses. These amendments, later known as the Bill of Rights, began with the First Amendment, which says, "Congress shall make no law respecting an establishment of religion, or prohibiting the free exercise thereof . . ." Clearly, the First Amendment was a restriction on Congress, not the states or any individual or group of individuals.

Several of the states had established churches that were similar to the Church of England. Virginia had just struggled free from the oppression of an established church where non-Anglicans experienced mild persecution. All of the colonists were familiar with the persecution and bloodshed resulting from overly zealous secular governments using coercion to force a state religion on their citizens.

After numerous attempts to draft language prohibiting the establishment of a national church, Madison wrote, "Congress shall make no law respecting an establishment of religion." He clearly meant a state church where ministers draw salaries from the government, bishops serve in the legislature, and people are taxed and otherwise burdened to support the established church's buildings, employees, and activities.

So the First Amendment prohibits the national Congress from

establishing a national religion, sponsored and funded by the national government, or from "prohibiting the free exercise thereof." Clearly, the national government (and its agencies) is not allowed to hinder, fine, imprison, or unduly restrict citizens in their expression of religion. There is no debate here regarding the prohibition. But this in no way undermines the fact that Christianity was by design part of the very fabric of the new federal government. And we should note that it was this new government, established on Christian principles, not on humanistic ideals, that created unprecedented freedoms for all religious faiths.

In the next chapter, I will show how the United States Supreme Court and lesser federal courts have used this First Amendment establishment of religion prohibition, which actually dealt with the role of Congress, to launch a vicious vendetta against all forms of public affirmation of faith in our nation.

THE "ESTABLISHMENT CLAUSE"

How did the first Congress regard the First Amendment establishment of religion clause? They treated it as the language specified, and they took great pains not to set up a national church.

On entering the newly formed House of Representatives, James Madison, who had written the First Amendment, served as chairman of the committee to choose a *paid* chaplain to open each session of the House with prayer. Madison, who knew better than anyone the constitutional prohibition against an "establishment of religion," clearly did not feel that using public funds to pay a Christian chaplain to lead the Congress in prayer in any way violated the prohibition.

Nor did the vote in the Continental Congress to appropriate funds to pay for the importing of 20,000 Bibles (due to what the Library of Congress records as a shortage caused by the Revolutionary War) violate what later became the First Amendment. Nor did the use of the Capitol Rotunda for Christian Sunday worship services appear in any way to establish a religion in contravention of the First Amendment.

As Thomas Jefferson put it in his second inaugural address, "I have not attempted to prescribe any form of worship for the federal government, but I have left the matter as the Constitution found it *with the states and the several religious bodies*" (emphasis added). Implicit in this remark is the sense that Thomas Jefferson could, if he had so desired, set up a form of worship for federal employees in the new central government without that act being considered an "establishment of religion."

The founding fathers recognized that religious faith was the essential underpinning of this new nation. In 1798 John Adams, who some consider the chief architect of the Constitution, remarked, "We have no government armed with power capable of contending with human passions unbridled by morality and religion. Avarice, ambition, revenge, or gallantry would break the strongest cords of our Constitution as a whale goes through a net. Our Constitution is designed only for a moral and religious people. It is wholly inadequate for any other."

Adams recognized that the "unbridled passions" of unregenerate people could only be controlled by the force of tyranny. Democratic self-government with maximum freedom was only possible to people who had restrained their basic instincts by self-regulating morality and religious belief.

OUR FOUNDERS AND THEIR FAITH

Our first president, George Washington, was a dedicated Christian, and he echoed the sentiment of Adams in his farewell address when he said, "Reason and experience both forbid us to expect that national morality can prevail in exclusion of religious principle."

In short, it was clear to the wise leaders at the founding of the

United States that the fear of God and the restraining hand of God's commandments prohibit people from murder, theft, adultery, immorality, perjury, and rebellion by the young. The generations of those who laid the legal, economic, and moral foundation of this land knew well the warning of King Solomon, who had written, "Without a vision of God, the people run amok" (Proverbs 29:18, author's translation). Without such a vision of a Creator—of ultimate reward and ultimate punishment—only martial law and armed restraint can prevent anarchy and mayhem.

Following the establishment of the federal union, each state adopted its own constitution. The constitution of every one of our fifty states includes a reference to God or Almighty God or divine guidance. Without question, the God referred to is not Allah or Brahma or Shiva or the Great Spirit. It is the Jehovah God of the Old and New Testaments. None of these Christian references has, to my knowledge, been challenged as an "establishment of religion." Each clearly indicates that the veneration of the Creator God is an integral part of the fabric of this nation.

I am including the references from the state constitutions in the appendix of this book. For illustration, here are a few of the references (emphases added):

CALIFORNIA

(Preamble)—We, the People of the State of California, *grateful to Almighty God for our freedom, in order to secure and perpetuate its blessings,* do establish this Constitution.

COLORADO

(Preamble)—We, the people of Colorado, *with profound reverence for the Supreme Ruler of the Universe,* in order to form a more independent and perfect government; establish justice; insure tranquility; provide for the common defense;

promote the general welfare and secure the blessings of liberty to ourselves and our posterity, do ordain and establish this constitution for the "State of Colorado."

FLORIDA

(Preamble)—We, the people of the State of Florida, *being grateful to Almighty God for our constitutional liberty,* in order to secure its benefits, perfect our government, insure domestic tranquility, maintain public order, and guarantee equal civil and political rights to all, do ordain and establish this constitution.

ILLINOIS

(Preamble)—We, the People of the State of Illinois— *grateful to Almighty God for the civil, political and religious liberty which He has permitted us to enjoy and seeking His blessing upon our endeavors*—in order to provide for the health, safety and welfare of the people; maintain a representative and orderly government; eliminate poverty and inequality; assure legal, social and economic justice; provide opportunity for the fullest development of the individual; insure domestic tranquility; provide for the common defense; and secure the blessings of freedom and liberty to ourselves and our posterity—do ordain and establish this Constitution for the State of Illinois.

IOWA

(Preamble)—We the people of the state of Iowa, *grateful to the Supreme Being for the blessings hitherto enjoyed, and feeling our dependence on Him for a continuation of those blessings,* do ordain and establish a free and independent government, by the name of the State of Iowa.

MASSACHUSETTS

... We, therefore, the people of Massachusetts, *acknowledging, with grateful hearts, the goodness of the great Legislator of the universe, in affording us, in the course of His providence,* an opportunity, deliberately and peaceably, without fraud, violence or surprise, of entering into an original, explicit, and solemn compact with each other; and of forming a new constitution of civil government, for ourselves and posterity; and devoutly imploring His direction in so interesting a design, do agree upon, ordain and establish the following *Declaration of Rights, and Frame of Government,* as the Constitution of the Commonwealth of Massachusetts.

(Article II)—It is the right as well as the duty of all men in society, publicly, and at stated seasons to *worship the Supreme Being, the great Creator and Preserver of the universe. And no subject shall be hurt, molested, or restrained, in his person, liberty, or estate, for worshipping God in the manner and season most agreeable to the dictates of his own conscience;* or for his religious profession or sentiments; provided he doth not disturb the public peace, or obstruct others in their religious worship.

(Article III)—*As the happiness of a people, and the good order and preservation of civil government, essentially depend upon piety, religion and morality; and as these cannot be generally diffused through a community, but by the institution of the public worship of God, and of public instructions in piety, religion and morality:* Therefore, to promote their happiness and to secure the good order and preservation of their government, the people of this commonwealth have a right to invest their legislature with power to authorize and require, and *the legislature shall, from time to time, authorize and require, the several towns, parishes, precincts, and other bodies politic, or religious societies, to make suitable provision, at their own expense, for the institution of the public worship of God, and for the support and maintenance of public Protestant teachers or piety, religion and morality, in all cases where such provision shall not be made voluntarily.*

OHIO

(Preamble)—We, the people of the State of Ohio, *grateful to Almighty God for our freedom, to secure its blessings and promote our common welfare,* do establish this Constitution.

This was America from its founding, through its revolution, through its growth from East to West, and to its rise as the most powerful nation on earth. America was a nation whose institutions, according to the Supreme Court case of *Zorach v. Clausen* in 1952, "presuppose the existence of a Supreme Being."

Despite injustice, despite corruption and bribery, despite a bloody Civil War, despite Reconstruction, this nation assented to a belief in Almighty God, to Jesus Christ as the Son of God, to the Holy Bible, and to the Ten Commandments of God as the acknowledged standard of human conduct.

We will see in the next chapter how a tiny minority of so-called elite, secular liberals decided to make a sneak attack on the source of American greatness by using the courts to destroy our spiritual heritage.

Two

Undermining a Nation's Foundation

To consider the judges as the ultimate arbiters of all constitutional questions [is] a very dangerous doctrine indeed, and one that would place us under the depotism of an oligarchy.

—THOMAS JEFFERSON (1820)

A GREAT DEAL IS MADE TODAY of the separation of powers established by the Constitution between the legislative, the executive, and the judiciary branches. The most casual reading of the Constitution shows where its framers placed major emphasis. The first article deals with the legislature itself: how the body is to be organized, how members are selected, and what powers they are to have. The Constitution gives Congress ultimate power over raising taxes and spending money. Congress was given the power to impeach the chief executive or any federal judge. By a simple majority vote, Congress could set the number of judges on the Supreme Court, establish such inferior courts as it felt appropriate, and determine the appellate jurisdiction of the Supreme Court.

In total, the framers devoted approximately 2,700 words in the Constitution to the legislature. Without a doubt, the framers of the Constitution intended that the Congress, which was the most representative of all the people, was to have the predominant power in the new central government. That is why the First Amendment in the Bill of Rights restricts the power of Congress, not that of the president or the courts.

When the framers got to Article III, establishing a federal judiciary, it was almost like an afterthought. Section 1 of Article III contains a scant 67 words. Section 2 contains 215 words. That was it: 282 words for the judiciary and some 2,700 for the legislature. It is informative to note that John Jay, the first Chief Justice, must have considered his office on the Court as part-time because he served at the same time as United States Ambassador to Great Britain. Ask yourself, which was more important in the original intention of the framers?

THE COURT'S LIMITED MANDATE

The Constitution established the Supreme Court to hear disputes arising from the lower courts that "Congress may from time-to-time ordain and establish." The judicial power was "to extend to all cases, in law and equity, arising under the Constitution, the laws of the United States, and treaties." The courts were to consider cases between states or in which the United States was a party. Certain cases, in what is known as original jurisdiction, were to go directly to the Supreme Court. The Supreme Court had appellate jurisdiction in law and fact, *"but only under such exceptions and regulations as Congress shall make."*

In sum, the courts were established to hear cases brought by plaintiffs against defendants. The number of Supreme Court judges could be set by Congress and was, in fact, set from seven to nine, then back to seven, then back to nine. The salaries of judges were set by Congress. The nature of appellate jurisdiction could be limited by Congress. The entire court system, under the Supreme Court, was to be established by a simple majority vote of Congress. The courts were to serve the people and their Congress, rather than the people being subservient to the courts.

JUSTICE MARSHALL'S POWER GRAB

Under no intelligent reading of the Constitution could any rational person come away with a view that the framers intended for the federal court system, which in large measure was to be a creation of Congress, to somehow morph itself into a super-legislature capable of nullifying at will the actions of the people's Congress.

Yet this is precisely what has happened over the history of the nation. The fourth chief justice was John Marshall of Virginia—a man of towering intellect and equally towering ambition. He found his chance to expand the power of the federal judiciary in an obscure case decided in 1803 called *Marbury v. Madison.*

The matter at issue hardly seemed earth shattering. William Marbury, who had been promised a commission as justice of the peace by the previous administration, sued President Thomas Jefferson's administration when it failed to make the appointment. Marbury did not file his action in the lower courts, but went directly to the Supreme Court, requesting an order to force James Madison—Jefferson's secretary of state—to deliver the commission by awarding Marbury a writ of mandamus (an order to force Madison to deliver the commission). The Court had been granted jurisdiction by Congress over such actions. But Marshall ruled otherwise.

Marshall said that Madison should have given the appointment, but then he held that the section of the Judiciary Act of 1789 that gave the Supreme Court original jurisdiction to issue writs of mandamus exceeded the authority allotted the Court under Article III of the Constitution and was therefore null and void. The Judiciary Act was ruled *unconstitutional.* Marshall then skillfully (some might say, deviously) said that the Court lacked the constitutional authority to issue the requested mandamus and therefore could not force the administration to make the appointment. Marshall was thus able to chastise the Jefferson administration and yet save himself and the

Court the embarrassment of being defied by Madison, who would have ignored the order had the Court tried to force compliance.

At the time, Marshall's ruling did not engender widespread opposition. After all, an obscure law case about an arcane action dealing with a low-level federal employee is hardly front-page news. In fact, it was not until 1857 that another act of Congress was declared unconstitutional. However, the poisonous seed was planted. And as we shall see, during the twentieth century, especially the last fifty years, the Supreme Court's exercise of powers *not* granted by the Constitution has accelerated at a disastrous rate. It now claims not only to have absolute authority to declare acts of Congress (and, by implication, acts of the president) unconstitutional, but to be the final authority on what the Constitution itself means.

PRESIDENTS FIGHT FOR RELIGION

Until the decision in *Marbury v. Madison*, each president and each member of Congress, since he or she had taken an oath to defend the Constitution, was considered perfectly capable of deciding constitutional interpretation. I have in my library selected writings of the early presidents. One veto message is particularly informative. President James Monroe went into great detail in analyzing the reasons that a proposed law establishing a particular road system fell outside the constitutional limits of the federal government. Nowhere in this message was the thought that the matter should be referred to the Supreme Court for a decision. To President Monroe, his oath was every bit as valid as the oath of each Supreme Court justice.

Yet the poisonous seed grew until the nation began to believe that a majority of nonelected judges (first four, then five) had power to trump the considered judgment of the elected representatives of the entire nation.

Thomas Jefferson fought Marshall's power grab bitterly. In 1820 he wrote, "To consider the judges as the ultimate arbiters of all constitutional questions [is] a very dangerous doctrine indeed, and one that would *place us under the despotism of an oligarchy.* Our judges are as honest as other men and not more so. They have with others the same passions for party, for power, and the privilege of their corps.... Their power [is] the more dangerous as they are in office for life and not responsible, as the other functionaries are, to the elective control. The Constitution has erected no such single tribunal, knowing that to whatever hands confided, with the corruptions of time and party, its members would become despots" (emphasis added).

Much later, Abraham Lincoln voiced the same warning when in his inaugural address he declared, "... The candid citizen must confess that if the policy of the government, upon vital questions, affecting the whole people, is to be irrevocably fixed by decisions of the Supreme Court, the instant they are made, in ordinary litigation between parties, in personal actions, the people will have ceased to be their own rulers, having, to that extent, practically resigned their government into the hands of that eminent tribunal."

Thankfully for the nation, during the nineteenth century and well into the twentieth century, judges exercised restraint. The power they had seized was employed to interpret the Constitution, not to rewrite it. The rule before the Court was the letter of the Constitution, the interpretation given in the Federalist Papers, and historic actions that would show what is called the "original intent" of the framers of the Constitution.

JUDGES TO RULE THE NATION

But humility and restraint finally gave way to arrogance. Consider the statement of Justice Charles Evans Hughes, made on May 3, 1907, before the Chamber of Commerce of Elmira, New York: "We are under a Constitution, but the Constitution is what the judges say it is." Like the priests at the Oracle of Delphi, black-robed justices now felt that only they had the secret to the mysteries. The Constitution was no longer what the framers had intended. It was whatever a majority of judges said it was at any given point of time.

It didn't take long for radical academics to realize that although Christian America would never vote for a radical secular agenda, just such an agenda could be imposed on America by action of the courts. It would only take an aggressive plaintiff with a facile left-wing legal team versus some less skilled and underpaid state official to gain a decision from five of nine judges that would undercut centuries of Christian public affirmation of faith. That is precisely how in 1963, radical atheist Madalyn Murray O'Hair was able to remove Bible reading from the schools of America. The case was a setup. The brief written by an assistant attorney general defending Bible reading in the schools of the state of Pennsylvania was so pitiful that, in my opinion, a high school senior with no legal training could have done a better job.

There was no vote by a majority of the people of Pennsylvania, and certainly not by the people of America. There was scarce representation for the defense by any highly skilled constitutional lawyers. Yet, despite 340 years of biblical education of our children, one atheist and a handful of judges stripped the Bible from all the schools of the nation. The moral education of our children was trampled underfoot by a tiny left-wing minority.

There are few lawyers educated in the United States during the past sixty years who have not been given the concept of judicial supremacy as a fundamental principle of constitutional law. I entered Yale Law School almost fifty years ago and studied constitutional law in my first year. At no time during that course did we analyze the text of the Constitution or the writings of the framers and their contemporaries. The first case in our casebook was *Marbury v. Madison*. From then on, we learned the landmark Supreme Court cases, which assumed without question the validity of the power grab by the Court.

STRIPPING THE NATION OF FAITH

Presumably my experience has been replicated in law schools across the land, which drill into students the supremacy of the Supreme Court. The liberal elites—the academics, the think tanks, the press, the big foundations, and, of course, the judges—do not want true democracy in America. They want a pliable judicial oligarchy that will strip any public affirmation of the Christian faith from our nation and in its place put the religion of secular humanism. Simultaneously, these same humanists grant constitutional protection to actions and lifestyles that for centuries have been and are still considered by most citizens to be both immoral and illegal.

Here's how the Supreme Court grew its power. In the case of *Marbury v. Madison* in 1803, the Supreme Court first declared an act of Congress unconstitutional. The *Scott v. Sandford* case in 1857 was the second. In cases decided between 1857 and 1900, the Supreme Court declared twenty-one acts of the United States Congress unconstitutional. Then judicial activism shifted into high gear between 1900 and 2000 when, in a staggering 129 cases, the Supreme Court declared acts of Congress unconstitutional. As I write this, the American Civil Liberties Union (ACLU) is petitioning a federal district judge in San Francisco to declare unconstitutional a congressional ban on partial-birth abortion. Not merely the Supreme Court, but now one district court judge is being asked to exercise power greater than that of the elected majority of both Houses of the United States Congress.

What is happening here is baffling to the nations of the world. It has come to be called "the American disease."

The desperate fight over judicial nominees in the United States Senate underscores the insistence of the radicals that the courts belong to them and are their tools in a culture war to reshape American values. Nominees for seats on circuit courts are now being rejected if they are Christians or if they do not subscribe to the radical agenda of abortion on demand, homosexual rights, homosexual education and marriage, and, of course, the ongoing vendetta against Christian expression in the public arena.

SOME JUSTICES HOLD THE LINE

Despite its radical swing to the left in the latter half of the twentieth century, the Supreme Court was supportive of the religious tradition of our nation and of the Christian faith during the first 150 years of its existence .

John Jay, who was the first Chief Justice of the newly formed Supreme Court, wrote this: "Unto Him who is the author and giver of all good, I render sincere and humble thanks for His mercy and unmerited blessings, and especially for our redemption and salvation by His beloved Son. . . . Blessed be his holy name."

Justice Joseph Story, who served from 1812 to 1845, was a prolific writer off the bench. His multivolume *Commentaries on the Constitution of the United States* are the first commentaries written on the Constitution and stand as the definitive nineteenth-century interpretation of the Constitution. In a section in his *Commentaries* concerning the First Amendment religion clauses, Story addressed the relation between religion and the state. He wrote: "Probably at the time of the adoption of the Constitution, and the amendments to it . . . the general, if not the universal, sentiment in America was, that Christianity ought to receive encouragement from the state, so far as was not incompatible with the private rights of conscience, and the freedom of religious worship."

Story was saying that our founders, so often appealed to for the modern idea of strict separation between church and state, actually anticipated that government would encourage Christianity. For Story, the question was not whether government could foster religion, but how far government may rightfully go in fostering it. As he explained, the right of government to interfere in matters of religion was a foregone conclusion:

[T]he right of a society or government to interfere in matters of religion will hardly be contested by any persons, who believe that piety, religion, and morality are intimately connected with the well being of the state, and indispensable to the administration of civil justice. The promulgation of the great doctrines of religion, the being, and attributes, and providence of one Almighty God; the responsibility of him for all our actions, founded upon moral freedom and accountability; a future state of rewards and punishments; the cultivation of all the personal, social, and benevolent virtues;—these never can be a matter of indifference in any well ordered community. It is, indeed, difficult to conceive, how any civilized society can well exist without them. And at all events, it is impossible for those, who believe in the truth of Christianity, as a divine revelation, to doubt, that it is the especial duty of government to foster, and encourage it among all the citizens and subjects.

Story's opinion reveals much about the favored status Christianity enjoyed in nineteenth-century America, both culturally and legally.

STILL A CHRISTIAN NATION

In 1892, the Supreme Court issued a unanimous decision in the case of *Holy Trinity v. United States*, written by Justice David Brewer, that the United States is "a Christian nation."

Brewer said that America's status as a Christian nation made it virtually untenable that Congress would pass a law detrimental to Christian or any other religion. He cited the Declaration of Independence, the colonial charters, and numerous state constitutions (which I mentioned in chapter 1). He cited the influences of Christianity in the First Amendment establishment of religion clause and the fact that the Constitution exempts Sunday from the calculated days in which a president can approve or veto legislation. Summing up, Justice Brewer wrote, "There is no dissonance in these declarations. There is a universal language pervading them all, having one meaning; they affirm and reaffirm that this is a religious nation."

Then Justice Brewer turned his attention to "American life as expressed by its laws, its businesses, its customs, and its society." He wrote:

> The form of oath universally prevailing concluding with an appeal to the Almighty; the custom of opening sessions of deliberative bodies and most conventions with prayer; the prefatory words of all wills, "In the name of God, Amen;" the laws respecting the observance of the Sabbath, with the general cessation of all secular business, and the closing of courts, legislatures, and other similar public assemblies on that day; the churches and church organizations which abound in every city, town, and hamlet; the multitude of charitable organizations existing everywhere under Christian auspices; the gigantic missionary associations, with general support, and aiming to establish Christian missions in every quarter of the globe . . .

It may stun some Americans living at the beginning of the twenty-first century that only 112 years ago, a unanimous decision by the United States Supreme Court declared that *this is a Christian nation.*

THE IMPACT OF HUMANISM, LIBERALISM, AND COMMUNISM

During the first five decades of the twentieth century, the world experienced geopolitical, spiritual, and economic convulsions on a scale unlike any other in the life of the United States from the colonial days forward.

Two world wars brought on the wanton slaughter of some seventy million people. The world experienced its most devastating economic depression, which led to an intellectual revolt against capitalism and free enterprise. The alphabet soup of central New Deal agencies under Franklin Roosevelt stretched the central government/state relationship of our federal republic to its limits as the federal government introduced a massive welfare state, together with an expansion of the commerce clause of the Constitution, to give the federal government power broad enough to tell a Nebraska farmer how many pigs he could raise.

Along with the social and economic strains caused by two world wars with the intervening Great Depression—during which 25 percent of the workforce was unemployed—came an even more insidious evil: international communism.

Communism was not so much an economic system as a religion which substituted for Christianity the belief in a utopian vision of a workers' paradise. That paradise would be brought on by human effort, after the structures of the old system of government, family, private property, and religion had been destroyed. To the communist, there is no God, only the state controlled by a new man that had been freed from the shackles of what communists consider "bourgeois morality."

In the 1890s, the Christian church in Germany came to be dominated by what is called higher criticism. To theologians embracing such beliefs, the Holy Bible is not the inspired Word of God; it is a compilation of source documents known as "Q" for Quelle (source); "J" for Yahwistic; "D" for Deuteronomic; and "P" for Priestly. To them, the "historic Jesus" was unknown, therefore the New Testament accounts were essentially fables put together by some early "redactor." These humanistic teachers sowed liberal doctrine like poison from Europe to the United States.

By 1920, the major mainline U.S. Protestant denominations were given over to theological liberalism and watered-down belief systems. In their seminaries and positions of leadership, they seemed unwilling to contend for America's historic Christian foundation.

THE ACLU IS FORMED

While the leading churches were sinking into spiritual apostasy, in 1920 a small group—some of whom had been affiliated with the Communist Party—formed an organization called the American Civil Liberties Union, or ACLU. Its early leader announced in the 1930s that his goal was to make America a "workers' state."

Communists desired world domination, especially domination over the United States. Their literature made clear that the best way to take over the United States was to destroy American morality by undermining the family structure and the public affirmation of the Christian faith. The ACLU targeted the courts. Some leftists targeted the media. Other communists infiltrated the major philanthropic foundations.

Another prong of the liberal offensive was aimed at the schools. A document called the Humanist Manifesto was issued in 1933. It stated that humanists did not believe in a divine being, that they did not believe in any inspired book from a divine being, that ethics are situational, and that absolute truth does not exist but is relative to cultures. Humanists declared that they resisted any limitation on the expression of consensual human sexuality, and finally, that they, the American humanists, found common ground with socialists around the world.

One of the drafters of this Humanist Manifesto was John Dewey, a professor and later dean of Teachers College at Columbia University. Dewey trained thousands of teachers to be humanists and to embrace cultural relativism, situational ethics, socialist economics, and disdain for Christianity.

THE JEWISH BACKLASH TO ANTI-SEMITISM

Another phenomenon that came to affect American jurisprudence was the backlash against the anti-Semitism that had grown in Europe from the 1880s through the horrors of Hitler's "final solution" in the 1930s and 1940s. Successive pogroms had been launched against helpless Jews living in Russia and Poland by so-called Christian czars, princes, and nobles. Waves of Jewish refugees fled from these persecutions and made their way to America, where they enjoyed the freedom to use their work ethic and intellectual brilliance to rise from humble beginnings. They excelled in medicine, law, investment banking, journalism, entertainment, education, and philanthropy. Christian America was a great friend of the Jewish people.

Then came the Nazi Holocaust, in which satanic barbarism led to the arrest, torture, and annihilation of six million Jews. Regrettably, to the Jews, the Nazis were a distorted form of Christianity.

Some Jewish leaders in the United States, assuming that anti-Semitism had arisen in Europe in Christian countries, decided that the future safety of American Jews would exist only if secularism replaced Christianity in the public arena. Organizations such as the American Jewish Congress and the Anti-Defamation League were formed to further these aims.

Some ten years ago I was asked by former United States Senator Rudy Boschwitz to participate in a symposium at a Minnesota university to discuss America's support of Israel and the role of religion in public life. One of my opponents was a charming, gracious, and articulate Jewish rabbi who disagreed with much of what I had to say. I said to him, "The Old Testament is a charter given by God declaring the special status of the Jewish people. Why wouldn't you be delighted for schoolchildren to learn it?"

His answer surprised me. "The majority view in America is Christian, and I would rather the schools have no religion, even what supports us, than have the Christian view of it."

In the early 1980s, an official of the Anti-Defamation League appeared as a guest on my television program, *The 700 Club*. He steadfastly affirmed that, despite overwhelming evidence, America was never a Christian nation. He emphatically declared that the founders of the nation were not Christians but deists. Similarly, when an official of the Christian Coalition stated that America was a Christian nation, he was blasted in the popular press by the Anti-Defamation League and made to apologize for "being insensitive to Jewish concerns."

It is easy to sympathize with the lonely Jewish student in a public school forced to sing Christmas carols and to listen to petitions to God that end "in Jesus's name." I have heard many touching stories about such people, especially in the South, who were asked to celebrate festivals and observances of a religion that they did not embrace.

THE WILL OF THE FEW

But is it fair or wise to take from the majority the celebration of Christmas, Good Friday, Easter, invocations at public gatherings, mention of God at public functions, or posting of the Ten Commandments, just to satisfy the requirements of a minority that wants no religion at all? Should any society give a veto over its cherished traditions and customs because a small group does not agree with them?

In cases involving free speech, the Supreme Court has repeatedly ruled that speech cannot be restricted because the speech may offend some or all of those who hear it. However, on matters of religion, all it takes is one complaining atheist to strip the majority of people in a community of their time-honored public affirmation of faith.

As a new century begins to unfold, new realities are emerging in which American evangelical Christians are seen as the most faithful supporters of Israel and Jewish causes. Orthodox Jews like the brilliant Rabbi Daniel Lapin decry the secularization of society. Lapin says openly that he would much prefer his children to live in a Christian America than a godless secular America, which tramples on the fundamental values he holds dear.

But are these sentiments too late to reverse the antireligious vendetta that the forces of militant secularism have urged for decades upon the Supreme Court and, in turn, our nation?

THE SEPARATION OF CHURCH AND STATE

With the decades of seething change in our society in the first half of the twentieth century, the Supreme Court took little action concerning religion until two cases: *Cantwell v. Connecticut* (1940) and *Everson v. Board of Education* (1947). Here is the backdrop against which these cases were decided.

Following the Civil War, Congress acted to ensure that slavery would forever be banished. The Thirteenth Amendment prohibited slavery and involuntary servitude. The Fourteenth Amendment gave every native-born or naturalized American dual citizenship in the nation and in their state of residence. It also forbade any state from "making or enforcing any law which shall abridge the privileges or immunities of citizens of the United States; nor shall any state deprive any person of life, liberty, or property, without due process of law; nor deny to any person within its jurisdiction the equal protection of the laws."

Shortly after the Fourteenth Amendment was ratified, U.S. Senator James G. Blaine offered in Congress what was known as the Blaine Amendment. This amendment sought to make the Fourteenth Amendment expand the First Amendment restrictions on the power of Congress and apply them to the states. That concept was hotly debated and rejected by a Congress that had recently passed the Fourteenth Amendment by a two-thirds vote. In other words, those who passed the Fourteenth Amendment never intended it to incorporate the First Amendment and apply it to the states.

But such a clear sense of original intent was insufficient to deter an activist Supreme Court. In the years immediately following World War II, in the cases of *Cantwell v. Connecticut* and *Everson v. Board of Education,* the Court applied by its own authority the First Amendment's Free Exercise and Establishment Clauses, not just to Congress, but to the states as well.

Now the Court was in position to address constitutional questions regarding religion, not only at the federal level, but in each of the fifty states. That was momentous. The use of prayers, oaths, chaplains, Bible reading, posting of the Ten Commandments, and holiday observances were now at the mercy of the federal judiciary. This was never intended by the framers.

There has never been a constitutional mandate for the "separation of church and state." Such language simply does not appear in the United States Constitution. It was the stated belief of our nation's framers and founders that the body politic received positive benefits from the religious life of its people and, therefore, religion was to be endorsed and encouraged at every level of government. Congress opens with prayer led by government-paid chaplains. The Supreme Court opens its daily session with prayer. Christianity and its customs were interwoven into every facet of the life of the United States of America from 1607 until 1947, a period of 340 years.

Yet in 1947, in *Everson v. Board of Education,* the Supreme Court lifted wording from a letter written by a man who had not participated in the drafting of the United States Constitution, stating in an offhand manner that government should keep its hands off the free exercise of religion. This personal letter, written in 1804 by Thomas Jefferson to the Danbury Baptist Convention, certainly did not have the force of law, nor could it approach in significance the commentaries of Supreme Court Justice Story or the majority decision of the Supreme Court in the *Trinity Trustees* (1892) case. Yet the Supreme Court lifted a phrase from Jefferson's letter—"wall of separation between church and state"—and used it to promulgate a radical new doctrine of constitutional law mandating an absolute separation of not just church, but also religion and state. Now by its own authority, never authorized by Congress, the Court transferred a prohibition against the congressional establishment of a national church to a prohibition against any religious acts by the state governments or their agents. In fact, before the Court had finished its absurd course, it even prohibited the state of North Carolina from printing a prayer for safety on its road maps.

340 Years of Law Tossed Aside

Just think, 340 years of clear law and practice supporting Christianity were tossed aside by the stroke of a simple majority of non-elected judges.

The *Everson* decision said that the Jefferson letter meant that government could neither "pass laws which aid one religion, aid all religions, or prefer one religion over another," nor could any government levy a "tax in any amount, large or small . . . to support any religious activities or institutions." The court closed with these words: "The First Amendment has erected a wall between church and state. That wall must be kept high and impregnable. We could not approve the slightest breach."

Obviously, the history of the First Amendment and the customs of early Supreme Courts and Congresses in no way support this unbelievably broad assertion. But the modern Court had said it, and, with the liberal left trumpeting the correctness of the decision, the public affirmation of the Christian faith in America was dealt what was to become a profound blow.

Everson was decided in 1947. By 1962 and 1963, the Court's hostility to religion accelerated dramatically in two cases that not only enraged Christians, but at the same time led to a demonstrable and precipitant acceleration of social pathologies—crime, drug abuse, teenage pregnancy, divorce, and alcoholism—throughout our land. From 1962 to 1963 onward, the statistics recording these social ills jumped to alarming levels. In fact, the clear legacy of the Supreme Court's hostility toward religious observance in the schools is the fact that by the late twentieth century the United States led the world in virtually every social pathology: the percentage of the population in prison, the percentage of teen pregnancy in the fully industrialized world, the consumption of illegal narcotics, the percentage of marriages ending in divorce, and the numbers of fatal shootings. Among advanced nations, France and the United States led in the percentage of the population who are alcoholics. And in scholastic achievement, the children of this once highly educated nation rated last among advanced nations in reading and verbal skills and in the bottom five in math skills.

To paraphrase the prophet Hosea, "The Supreme Court has sown the wind; the nation has reaped the whirlwind."

PRAYER IS THE FIRST TO GO

The first of these antireligious decisions was *Engel v. Vitale* (1962), a case that challenged the long-held custom of schoolchildren in New York reciting each day a prayer that had been composed by the New York educational supervisory body, the New York Board of Regents. The court ruled that this prayer violated the *Everson* standard of the supposed "constitutional wall of separation between church and state."

The lone dissenter was Justice Potter Stewart, who wrote that in denying "the wish of those schoolchildren to join in reciting this prayer," the Court was denying them the opportunity in "sharing the spiritual heritage of our nation." Stewart continued, "I cannot see how an 'official religion' is established by letting those who want to say a prayer say it."

Justice Stewart said that to treat a simple prayer the same as the establishment and patronage of a church by the federal government makes a mockery of the dangers the First Amendment was aimed at preventing. Saying prayers before school, according to Stewart, is no different than saying prayers to open the sessions of Congress or the Supreme Court itself. These practices, he said, "recognize and . . . follow the deeply entrenched and highly cherished spiritual traditions of our nation—traditions which came down to us from those who almost two hundred years ago avowed their firm reliance on the protection of divine providence when they proclaimed the freedom and independence of this brave new world."

The Supreme Court in *Engel* did not just strike down the voluntary recitation of a prayer at a public school; it struck at the very heart of the spiritual heritage of the nation.

BIBLE READING IS NEXT TO GO

Following hard after *Engel v. Vitale* in 1962 was the Pennsylvania Bible reading case known as *Abington School District v. Schempp*, decided in 1963. In the *Schempp* case, the Court struck down the voluntary practices of Bible reading and reciting the Lord's Prayer in public schools. In so doing, the Court eliminated practices that the founders of the public school system considered to be indispensable to the highest welfare of the students and "essential to the vitality of moral education."

A commentary on the writing of Horace Mann, the father of public education, noted that the entire curriculum of the public schools centered on the general assumptions of God's existence, the sense of His universe, and the spirituality of human nature. "The system," according to Mann, "earnestly inculcates all Christian morals; it founds its morals on the basis of religion, it welcomes the religion of the Bible; and in receiving the Bible it allows it to speak for itself."

Justice Potter Stewart dissented vigorously against the majority decision in the Bible reading case:

It might also be argued that parents who want their children exposed to religious influences can adequately fulfill that wish off school property and outside school time. With all its surface persuasiveness, however, this argument seriously misconceives the basic constitutional justification for permitting [Bible reading in public schools]. For a compulsory state educational system so structures a child's life that if religious exercises are held to be an impermissible activity in schools, religion is placed at an artificial and state-created disadvantage. Viewed in this light, permission of such exercises for those who want them is necessary if the schools are truly to be neutral in the matter of religion. And a refusal to permit religious exercises thus is seen not as the realization of state neutrality, but rather as the *establishment of a religion of secularism.* (emphasis added)

Justice Stewart got it right. Not only was the Court undermining the essential moral underpinnings of our public education, it was doing precisely what John Dewey and his fellow humanists had been advocating since 1930—the establishment in the public schools of the religion of secular humanism with its attendant sexual permissiveness, embrace of one world government, and Marxist-inspired economic theory.

ANTIRELIGION BIAS SHOWS

Conservative judges on the Court are speaking out about the anti-religious bias of the Court in recent decades. In the *Santa Fe Independent School District v. Doe* case decided in 2000, the Court struck down prayers at high school football games in which the prayers had been decided upon by a majority of students who were free to vote for prayer, against prayer, about who should pray, and about what should be prayed. It was again incredible to believe that such a simple religious observance under these auspices could, by even the wildest flight of fancy, be considered the establishment of a state-sponsored religion. But in matters of religion, the Court's decision, to quote Chief Justice Rehnquist's blistering dissent in the *Santa Fe* case, "bristles with hostility to all things religious in public life."

I have shown the heartrending social pathologies that resulted from the Supreme Court's ruthless dismantling of the nation's historical school-based religious instruction. We may never fully realize the damage to our national psyche and our standing in the world as a bastion of freedom and righteousness.

The U.S. Supreme Court has raised its fist and shaken it in the face of Almighty God. And "Christian America" and our leadership let it happen. Do we suppose that we will be spared the judgment of a righteous God just because we mouth religious platitudes and sing "God Bless America"?

What other outrage has the tyrannical majority on the Supreme Court been guilty of, and what can we do to stop it?

THREE

Supreme Court v. Ten Commandments

Posting of religious texts on the wall serves no . . . educational function. If the posted copies of the Ten Commandments are to have any effect at all, it will be to induce the children to read, meditate upon, perhaps to venerate and obey the Commandments . . . [This] is not a permissible state objective under the Establishment Clause.
—Justice Paul Stevens
for the majority in *Stone v. Graham* (1980)

IF YOU WERE TO ASK where the American concepts of right and wrong came from, the most common answer would undoubtedly be the Bible. If you pressed further for more specifics, the answer in most instances would be the Ten Commandments or the Sermon on the Mount. Ask any historian to name the source of the legal concepts underlying the criminal laws of Western civilization, and a substantial majority would say either the Law of Moses or the Ten Commandments.

The chief justice of the current Supreme Court, William Rehnquist, declared, "The secular application of the Ten Commandments is clearly seen in its adoption *as the fundamental legal code of Western Civilization and the Common Law of the United States"* (emphasis added).

Consider our laws that prohibit the taking of an innocent life. We regard murder as heinous. We debate motives for killing, issues of premeditation, and forensic evidence that either points to guilt or innocence. Then with eyes agog, we stare for hours at the legal maneuverings in the murder trials of the O. J. Simpsons and Scott

Petersons, and the nation becomes a great jury to convict or acquit. We are shown endless episodes of television shows like *Law and Order,* in which the hard-charging prosecuting attorney talks each week about making a deal with the accused for "man one" or "man two" (for first- or second-degree manslaughter).

Most civilized people have innate respect for human life, but where do we get our notions that killing another human being is wrong? The answer is very simple: from the Sixth Commandment, "Thou shalt not kill" (Exodus 20:13 KJV).

WHY ALL THE VIOLENCE?

I recall a news account some years ago of a gang of teenage hoodlums in Southern California who invaded the stands at a Friday night high school football game. They picked out a handsome young couple and proceeded to gun down the boy in cold blood. There was no provocation. No revenge. No turf battle. Just cold-blooded killing for the thrill of the experience.

The three hoodlums fled the stadium before security could intervene. What happened next sends chills down my spine. They calmly entered a fast-food restaurant three blocks away and ordered double cheeseburgers, French fries, and cokes. Then they laughed about how their victim had gurgled on his own blood while he was dying from the wounds they had inflicted.

Think of it: going to town on Friday night for sport, killing a promising young teenager, and then spending the remainder of the evening wolfing down double cheeseburgers and regaling one another with the victim's death agonies. No twinge of conscience. No remorse. No sense that they had done anything wrong.

In the 1970s, David Wilkerson, the founder of Teen Challenge, wrote of a vision he said he received from the Lord. Part of this vision centered on the terror that would be loosed on our cities by preteens and teenagers who were born out of wedlock or who had little or no parental love and discipline. According to Wilkerson, these youngsters would grow up wild, with no discipline and no natural affection, and they would begin to terrorize our cities with murder, rape, robbery, and mayhem.

Surely the young killers in Southern California lived up to the description of the wild youth of Wilkerson's "vision."

Only an old man wearing a long black robe, totally detached from reality, could have possibly written that teaching our young people that their Creator commands them not to kill would have "no educational function," or, for that matter, no secular purpose.

WHAT WILL BE THE FATE OF OUR CHILDREN?

In days gone by, it was assumed that schools were to be the conduits of the ethical and moral principles of our nation to the next generation. Without question, the nation believed that stealing and murder and perjury were wrong. Our criminal laws imposed stiff penalties for those who violated these norms. And isn't it far superior to tell students that there is a Higher Power who is the ultimate impartial Lawgiver, that there is ultimate reward and punishment for our actions here on earth, and that our legal standards of right and wrong are not merely the creation of the all-too-fallible Democratic or Republican majority of the legislature?

Some years ago I hosted a segment on my television program, *The 700 Club*, about ethical education in the schools of a major county in Georgia. My guests were three public school teachers. One of them told me of a teachers' instruction guide published by the National Education Association and approved for use in the high schools of the school district.

In the teacher's manual was this question: "What do you say if a student asks you if shoplifting is wrong?" The approved answer should shock you as much as it shocked me: "I cannot tell you if shoplifting is right or wrong; you must decide for yourself."

I exploded with indignation. "If that kid is caught shoplifting, he will go to jail. How dare the schools set these students up to commit crime like that!" Of course, the teachers had no answer.

But this is the situational ethics and cultural relativism of John Dewey run amuck. The commandments of God are absolute, not situational. The Eighth Commandment says, "Thou shalt not steal" (Exodus 20:15 KJV), not "You have to determine for yourself if stealing is wrong, depending on the situation and the culture." Is there not an educational benefit to be derived from teaching children not to steal? A majority of the Supreme Court finds no benefit in obedience to such a commandment.

In our television news at CBN, we like to take the pulse of ordinary people on the streets of cities and towns. What people say in pop interviews is informative and interesting. One of our reporters was given an assignment to test the attitudes of typical high school teenagers regarding moral and ethical issues. What she discovered was the following pattern:

> *Question:* Is killing right or wrong?
> *Answer:* It depends. Perhaps it might be a good thing to
> help a person to be killed.

A study of teenage attitudes was released several years ago by a popular teen magazine. On a scale of one to ten, an overwhelming majority of the teens interviewed felt that using a parking space reserved for the handicapped was much worse than premarital sex.

With an explosion of inner-city, out-of-wedlock births at over 70 percent; with the welfare rolls bursting because of the poverty of single women with children; with over three million teenagers contracting some form of sexually transmitted disease each year; how can the Supreme Court say that teaching the Ten Commandments has no educational value for today's schoolchildren?

The Seventh Commandment says, "Thou shalt not commit adultery" (Exodus 10:14 KJV). Will not homes be stronger, society be stronger, children be better cared for, and poverty be reduced if that commandment is followed? How dare Justice Stevens declare that under our Constitution it is, effectively, impermissible for children to be taught marital fidelity!

CORRUPT TWENTY-FIRST-CENTURY BUSINESS ETHICS

For the past year, our newspapers and television news programs have been filled with shocking revelations of corporate fraud and deceptive behavior at major corporations such as Enron, World-Com, Adelphia, and Tyco. Some of our largest public auditors have been charged with obstruction of justice and run out of business.

Perhaps the most intriguing figure is Martha Stewart. Martha was a guest on my television program to demonstrate the secrets of preparing the perfect holiday meal. She was and is fascinating.

When she started her career, women could not get enough of Martha Stewart's decorating, cooking, and gardening tips. She was so popular that before long she not only had a regular television show, but a magazine and a line of home products, followed by a lucrative contract with a major retail chain. She formed a company, Martha Stewart Living Omnimedia, which was considered a growth company on the New York Stock Exchange. At one time, this daughter of poor immigrants held stock valued by the market at nearly one billion dollars.

Along the way, Martha Stewart purchased a relatively modest number of shares in a company called ImClone Systems, which had been founded by a physician who was a friend of her family. Im-Clone Systems had a fast run on the stock market because it held patents on a drug called Erbitux, which was supposed to cure certain cancers. Then the Food and Drug Administration declined to approve Erbitux and sent a notice to that effect to Sam Waksal, the founder of the company.

What happened next is open to speculation. Martha Stewart sold her ImClone stock. The price was around $300,000—which is pocket change for someone of Martha's wealth. She stated when questioned that she had placed a previous stop-loss order with her broker to sell when the stock of Imclone fell to sixty dollars per share. Later, a broker's assistant maintained that he had told Martha that the Waksals were selling and so should she.

In either case, Martha was not privy to what could be termed insider information. Even if she sold her stock after a tip from her broker, in the worst light it would be a civil offense requiring undue profits to be disgorged.

Apparently, though, the government was looking to convict a high-profile person like Martha Stewart, so they began a barrage of questioning. If she had said, "It's true. I got a call from my broker and sold my stock. So what?" some government accountant would have assessed a modest penalty and the case would have been over—or Martha could have possibly fought the penalty, won, and the case would have been closed.

However, she seemed to change stories under questioning. Suddenly, the federal investigators, who until this time had no case at all, could bring a criminal charge of perjury and obstruction of justice against Martha Stewart. Throughout America, this talented and successful woman was reviled and ridiculed in the press. The value of her stock plummeted, and with it, several hundred million dollars of Martha Stewart's net worth.

Mistakes, oversights, poor judgment, and even some illegal or immoral acts can be forgiven by the public, but if one lies to cover up bad behavior, the original act is magnified ten times over. Our culture still honors truth telling, so why on earth does the Supreme Court object to posting the Ninth Commandment—not to bear false witness—in public places?

Once again it becomes crystal clear that the tortured reasoning of the Supreme Court is not only at cross-purposes with God, but it puts our children in serious jeopardy before the laws of our land.

REMOVING THE TEN COMMANDMENTS

Virtually all Americans, along with Chief Justice Rehnquist, believe that the Ten Commandments form the basis of the moral and legal standards of the United States. So the Court's decision in the 1980 case of *Stone v. Graham* shocked the nation by striking down a Kentucky statute that required posting privately funded Ten Commandment displays "on the wall of each public classroom in the state."

The Kentucky legislature's avowed secular purpose for posting the Ten Commandments was clearly printed at the bottom of each display: "The secular application of the Ten Commandments is clearly seen in its adoption as the fundamental legal code of Western Civilization and the Common Law of the United States."

The Supreme Court dismissed this clear statement, declaring that "requiring the posting of the Ten Commandments in public schoolrooms has no secular legislative purpose and is therefore unconstitutional," under what is known as the "Lemon test" (from the standard of the Supreme Court case of *Lemon v. Kurzman* [1971]). The Court went on to say, "The pre-eminent purpose for posting the Ten Commandments on schoolroom walls is plainly religious in nature. The Ten Commandments are undeniably a sacred text in the Jewish and Christian faiths, and no legislative recitation of a supposed secular purpose can blind us to that fact."

This finding, according to the Chief Justice in his dissent, suggests an improper purpose on the part of the Court to insulate "the

public sectors . . . from all things which may have a religious significance or origin," especially those things that have their origin in
the Christian religion. Our nation's founders and the framers of our
Constitution would be horrified at the Court's ruling.

Our first president, the father of our country, and the presiding
officer at the convention that drafted the United States Constitution said it eloquently in his farewell address, which I once again
repeat: "Reason and experience both forbid us to expect that
national morality can prevail in exclusion of religious principle."

And again the words of John Adams: "We have no government
armed with power capable of contending with human passions
unbridled by morality and religion. Avarice, ambition, revenge, or
gallantry would break the strongest cords of our Constitution as a
whale goes through a net. Our Constitution is designed only for a
moral and religious people. It is wholly inadequate for any other."

The people and their elected representatives—comprising millions of individuals—realize that there can be no law and order,
no public morality, in the absence of religious principle. Yet the
Supreme Court majority—consisting of five individuals—has mandated that no governmental agency may bring to bear the restraining force of religious principle on the conduct of its citizens.

In short, in a society that is wallowing in sexual permissiveness,
drug addiction, broken homes, crime, and violence, the Supreme
Court forbids legislators to reach into the great religious heritage of
our nation to set forth for American citizens God's way to a better,
happier life.

THE ACLU AND PLANNED PARENTHOOD ATTACK

As if this secularization wasn't enough, consider two recent cases—
one in California by the ACLU, the other in Florida by Planned
Parenthood. Fortunately, the courts at this time were unwilling to

rule favorably on these outlandish motions, but the fact that lawyers would suggest such things shows how the ultra-left interprets the final logic of the Supreme Court's anti-God decisions.

In California, the ACLU sued to strike down as unconstitutional a California law promoting heterosexual, monogamous marriage. To the ACLU, heterosexual, monogamous marriage was a "religious" concept and therefore impermissible under recent Supreme Court rulings as an "establishment of religion."

The suit brought by Planned Parenthood in Duval County, Florida, was equally outlandish. The School Board of Duval County had introduced a course in the curriculum that encouraged sexual abstinence among unmarried teenagers. The lawyers for Planned Parenthood urged upon the lower court the premise that sexual abstinence is a "religious" concept; therefore, teaching sexual abstinence in public schools is unconstitutional.

Although these two plaintiffs were unsuccessful, it is easy to see the absurd results that the Supreme Court's reasoning can bring about. Almost all of our concepts of right and wrong come from religious sources. If every legislative initiative must be purely secular, then this nation will have lost the restraining religious principle underlying our laws, and one day in the distant future we may find ourselves open to lawless anarchy.

ASSAULTS ON THE TEN COMMANDMENTS

Another case involving the Ten Commandments, titled *Books v. Elkhart*, was decided in 2000. In the *Elkhart* case, the Supreme Court refused to consider a Seventh Circuit decision that a Ten Commandments monument that had been displayed for over forty years on the lawn of the Elkhart, Indiana, municipal building violated the Establishment Clause. Washington, Adams, and Jefferson would have thought that was ridiculous.

Once again, Chief Justice Rehnquist argued vigorously against the Court's refusal to hear the case. In his dissent he regarded as an accepted and unassailable law that a state is permitted a religious act only if it has a secular purpose and does not advance the cause of religion. As I have discussed above, these concepts are alien to the original intent of the framers of the Constitution.

Nevertheless, the Chief Justice wished to support the Elkhart monument. Here are his words:

> The city has displayed the monument outside the Municipal Building, which houses the local courts and local prosecutor's office. This location emphasizes the foundational role of the Ten Commandments in secular, legal matters. Indeed, a carving of Moses holding the Ten Commandments, surrounded by representations of other historical legal figures, adorns the frieze on the south wall of our courtroom, and we have said that the carving "signals respect not for great proselytizers but for great lawgivers." Similarly, the Ten Commandments monument and surrounding structures convey that the monument is part of the city's celebration of its cultural and historical roots, not a promotion of religious faith. To that end, the monument shares the lawn outside the Municipal Building with the Revolutionary War Monument, which honors the Revolutionary War soldiers buried in Elkhart County, and a structure called the "Freedom Monument" . . . I would grant certiorari to decide whether a monument which has stood for more than 40 years, and has at least as much civic significance as it does religious, must be physically removed from its place in front of the city's Municipal Building.

COURT LOGIC GONE MAD

But the words of the Chief Justice were not to prevail as the eighty-year-old Justice Stevens, continuing his vendetta against the Ten Commandments, wrote for the majority:

> The first two lines of the monument's text appear in significantly larger font than the remainder . . . These lines read: "The Ten Commandments—I Am The Lord Thy God." The graphic emphasis placed on those first lines is rather hard to square with the proposition that the monument expresses no particular religious preference . . . Moreover, three principal speakers at the monument's dedication had been a Catholic priest, a Protestant minister, and a Jewish rabbi . . . who spoke of the cross-cultural significance of the Ten Commandments.

Imagine, a religion is established when three clergymen speak of "crosscultural significance"!

Push the unbelievable logic of Stevens's argument much farther and the State of California will be forced to change the religious names of its three principal cities: Los Angeles (the angels), San Francisco (the Catholic Saint Francis), and Sacramento (the sacraments of the Christian church). Or should two cities named Santa Fe (holy faith) be forced by the Supreme Court to change their names for being religiously motivated? Or how about Los Cruces (the crosses) in New Mexico or the Sangre de Christo (blood of Christ) mountains, also in New Mexico? Perhaps the Court will next take aim at St. Louis, Missouri; or Zion, Illinois; or Bethlehem, Pennsylvania; or St. Paul, Minnesota; or St. Petersburg, Florida. Where could it ever end?

Frankly, we are left with the inescapable conclusion that either the majority of the Court is made up of illogical left-wing fanatics or people so trapped by their own convoluted reasoning that they don't see the emotional, political, and spiritual shipwreck they are slowly but surely bringing on this great nation.

THE CASE AGAINST JUDGE MOORE

As I write this book today, I am looking at the headline on an Associated Press story: "Supreme Court rejects church-state fight over Ten Commandments monument."

What was this dispute all about? Alabama state judge Roy Moore became famous after the Kentucky and Indiana cases by posting the Ten Commandments in his courtroom. The people of Alabama were furious at the treatment given their cherished religious symbols by the U.S. Supreme Court. Judge Moore became a hero throughout Alabama because of his defense of the Ten Commandments. In the following statewide election, Judge Moore was elected by a decisive majority as the next chief justice of the sovereign state of Alabama.

Shortly after assuming office, Chief Justice Moore, using private funds, caused a 5,200-pound granite monument to be carved to display the Ten Commandments. This monument was given a prominent place in the rotunda of the building that houses the Supreme Court of Alabama.

The people of Alabama were strongly supportive of Justice Moore's efforts, but the ACLU, which has declared itself opposed to every expression of religious faith in the public arena, brought a suit in the Montgomery federal district court to have the monument removed.

Since Moore was chief justice of the highest court in Alabama, and since the Alabama Constitution contained clear references to God, he considered it perfectly appropriate to have in his courthouse the same commandments that adorn the walls of the United States Supreme Court in Washington, D.C. Chief Justice Moore was certainly within his rights to question whether a federal district court judge had the power to order him to do anything.

The federal judge trying the case said that he did not know who or what God was, and then he speculated about a Hindu God or a Buddhist God or no God at all. The judge could have enlightened himself by looking at the reverse side of a United States one-dollar bill.

The U.S. District Court judge ordered the monument removed. Judge Moore appealed but, unfortunately, did not ask for a timely stay of the order, so it appeared that he was in contempt of court by not removing the monument as ordered. Therefore, he was suspended from his post by his Alabama colleagues. The monument was hauled away and dumped out of sight in a storeroom.

On November 13, 2003, Judge Moore was removed from the bench by the nine members of the Supreme Court for having "placed himself above the law."

"I have absolutely no regrets," Moore told supporters at the courthouse in Montgomery. "It's about whether or not you can acknowledge God as a source of our law and our liberty."

Judge Moore's case reveals the blatant hypocrisy of the U.S. Supreme Court. As Rob Schenck, president of the Washington-based National Clergy Council, declared to the Court, "If you can display these Ten Commandments above your head, why can't the people of Alabama display them in the rotunda of their Supreme Court building?"

SEARCH AND DESTROY THE TEN COMMANDMENTS

Emboldened by their success, the ACLU has asked their supporters to hunt down every display of the Ten Commandments for the purpose of eradicating them by judicial action. In the days of the ascendance of the worship of Baal in Israel, God raised up the prophet Elijah to hunt down and destroy the statues of Baal throughout God's land. Isn't it ironic in post-Christian America to find an organization mobilizing its forces to hunt down and destroy across our land one of the most prominent public symbols of the same God who showed His power against the priests of Baal in the days of Elijah?

It is abundantly clear from the facts of history that the Supreme

Court of the United States over the years has executed a judicial *coup d'état*. The judges have stolen power not granted them by the Constitution and used it for decades to wage a relentless and thoroughgoing war against the Judeo-Christian spiritual foundation of our nation.

In an address to the Intercollegiate Studies Institute on October 23, 2003, one of the conservative members of the Court, Antonin Scalia, ridiculed a recent Supreme Court ruling on consensual sodomy that, according to Scalia, "held to be a constitutional right what had been a criminal offense at the time of the founding and for nearly 200 years thereafter."

Scalia said judges, including his colleagues on the Supreme Court, throw over the original meaning of the Constitution when it suits them. "Most of today's experts on the Constitution think the document written in Philadelphia in 1787 was simply an early attempt at the construction of what is called a liberal political order," the Associated Press reported Scalia as saying. "All that the person interpreting or applying that document has to do is to read up on the latest academic understanding of liberal political theory and interpolate these constitutional understandings into the constitutional text."

BREAKING FREE FROM THE SUPREME COURT

So how do free people break themselves free from this black-robed bondage? What avenues are open?

Article XI of the United States Constitution states that the Constitution is the supreme law of the land. "All executive and judicial offices, both of the United States and of the several states, shall be bound by oath or affirmation, to support this Constitution."

The judges are not supporting or defending the Constitution; they are destroying its original meaning to make it say what its framers never intended. This in itself is grounds for impeachment. These judges have violated their oath and no longer can serve on "good behavior," as they declare in their oath of office.

Whether Congress has the will to act is problematic. Congress will only act if the people have become so outraged that their elected representatives once again take back the power given them under the Constitution.

Some of us can remember a similar effort in the 1960s when billboards across the land shouted "Impeach Earl Warren!" But in that era there was no groundswell in America against the excesses of the Warren Court. "Impeach Earl Warren" came to be regarded as the ravings of the loony fringe . . . never anything more.

Recently I was able to enlist 120,000 Christian people across America to petition the Supreme Judge of the universe for help. In what we called Operation Supreme Court Freedom, we asked God to spare this nation for our children and grandchildren by causing three liberal judges of the Supreme Court to retire. With God's help, the task is relatively simple.

WHO ARE THESE JUSTICES?

Justice Anthony Kennedy is a Catholic appointed to the Court by Ronald Reagan. Kennedy came to the bench as a conservative. Now he only occasionally votes for conservative causes. His denunciation of the graduation prayer by a rabbi in *Lee v. Weisman* (1992) was biting and far-reaching, and his written opinion for the majority declaring a constitutional right to sodomy in the case of *Lawrence v. Texas* (2003) reached giddy lyricism in support of the homosexual lifestyle. He not only departed from the Constitution, he declared that the reasoning of former Justice Lewis Powell in the previous Supreme Court case of *Bowers v. Hardwick* (1986), upholding a Georgia law against sodomy, was incorrect and should be reversed. In the process, he reached across the Atlantic to decisions of European courts in order to justify his abhorrent reasoning and nebulous concepts of personhood.

In many cases, such as those involving regulations restricting abortion protests and regulations against school Bible clubs, Kennedy forms part of a conservative bloc on the Court. In short, Kennedy is often driven by misguided liberalism and then on other occasions is motivated by a refreshing gust of common sense and justice.

When Ronald Reagan was contemplating the appointment of a woman to the Court, he settled on a Stanford Law schoolmate of Justice Rehnquist who had served as a Republican in the state senate of Arizona and later in the Arizona judiciary. Surely someone from Barry Goldwater's state would be conservative, but this was not the case.

I joined Paul Weyrich, the head of the Free Congress Foundation, for a private lunch with James Baker, Reagan's chief of staff. We sought to convince Baker that Sandra Day O'Connor was neither pro-life nor a strong conservative. Baker assured us that this lady was a "woman for all seasons" and that she would prove a splendid justice who enjoyed the full confidence of the president.

Baker was wrong. Justice O'Connor is pro-choice, and she is always a question mark or a vote against traditional values on religious issues. Justice O'Connor reportedly desires to step down from the Court and return to Arizona with her husband. If she is replaced with a strong judicial conservative who is dedicated to upholding the original intent of the Constitution, there will then be four solid votes for freedom from tyranny.

On the left is Justice Ginsberg, who was a former general counsel of the infamous ACLU. It boggles comprehension that a Senate controlled by Republicans could have allowed President Bill Clinton to appoint to the Court an avowed enemy of traditional values. Such an appointment is so egregious, and such a confirmation by the Senate so lacking in principle, that I find it hard to believe that there was not undue pressure behind the scenes.

Justice Stevens is eighty-three years old at this writing. His visceral hatred of our Christian religious tradition is clear from his written decisions. Were he to retire and be replaced by a justice with the conservative judicial philosophy of a Thomas or a Scalia, a host of erroneously decided cases could be reversed and this nation could finally be free from the tyranny of the judicial oligarchy.

REBUILDING THE SUPREME COURT

Since so much is at stake, the fight over the next three Supreme Court justices is going to be bitter and bloody. Ultra left-wing groups like People for the American Way, National Abortion and Reproductive Rights Action League, the National Organization of Women, the ACLU, and the Gay-Lesbian Alliance will use every dirty trick imaginable to smear the reputation of conservative nominees to the Court. The issue will depend on whether America's evangelical Christians and their allies have the stomach for a protracted and costly battle. Ronald Reagan once said, "In dealing with Congress, it is not necessary that they see the light, but that they feel the heat." Republican and Democrat members of the Senate need to realize that if they vote against confirmation of conservative judicial nominees, they will not be returned to office. There needs to be no quarter and no compromise.

We Americans have a great respect for law and order. The great Samuel Rutherford wrote *Lex Rex:* "The Law Is King." I once sat next to former British prime minister Margaret Thatcher at a private dinner in London. I asked, "Lady Thatcher, what should be done to correct the turmoil in Russia?"

Her answer was immediate. "They need English judges to teach them the rule of law."

We prize an independent judiciary, free from political pressure, to render dispassionate decisions that are guided by law and reason. The American people assume that judicial decisions are made fairly and according to the law. We do not have an arbitrary monarch claiming to rule by divine right. Our entire system of free enterprise is based on the concept of the rule of law, which upholds contract obligations and protects citizens from the arbitrary exercise of power by the strong.

Yet now in America the law is not king; judges have become king. What the Europeans call "the American disease" must be cured, and the people of America must again assert their authority.

A RADICAL SOLUTION

If appointments do not take place, the final course is to nullify the decisions of the Supreme Court. The Court has been given no army, no enforcement mechanism, and no ability to raise money. Supreme Court decisions carry weight only because they are given weight by the chief executive and his attorney general, and by federal marshals. The Supreme Court can't function if the Congress refuses to appropriate it any money beyond the salaries mandated by the Constitution.

If the chief executive declares that judicial decisions have overstepped constitutional limits and refuses to enforce them, then the decisions will have no effect except upon cases brought in lower courts. If Congress refuses to allow the Court to overturn laws that it has passed, then those laws will remain in effect. If Congress wishes to limit the jurisdiction of the Supreme Court over an entire class of cases, it may do so under the Constitution.

The Supreme Court has taken power unto itself because the other two branches of our government have refused to act. It will not precipitate a constitutional crisis if an arrogant usurper of power is forced to abide by the limits set for it by our founding fathers. Our existence as a free nation is at stake. Are we willing to act?

Now I turn from man-made law to the law of God, the Ten Commandments, which are being driven by the judiciary from our public square. What are these commandments, and why, to many, have they become "The Ten Offenses?"

FOUR

Commandment One: Worship the One True God

I am the LORD your God. . . .
Do not worship any other gods besides me.

—EXODUS 20:2–3 NLT

IMAGINE THE SCENE: Some 600,000 ragged Hebrew men, along with their families—all former slaves—were free from bondage after four hundred years of captivity in the land of Egypt. Their leader was a man named Moses, who, the record tells us, was raised by the daughter of Pharaoh, the ruler of Egypt. Moses was a prince of Egypt, a powerful warrior who was skilled in all the wisdom of the land. Raised in the palace of the ruler of the most powerful nation on earth, Moses had everything that a virile young man could want: money, power, servants, women, fame, unlimited opportunity, and possibly even a chance at the throne of Egypt as the son of Pharaoh's daughter.

As he grew older, Moses learned a bitter truth. He was not an Egyptian prince, but the son of a Hebrew named Amram. One day, Moses saw an Egyptian overseer beating a Hebrew unmercifully. In the ensuing struggle, Moses struck and killed the Egyptian. When he later learned that his deed was known, he left his royal heritage and fled for his life into the desert of Midian. There, at age forty, he married the daughter of Jethro, a priest and chief of Midian, and spent the next forty years tending sheep in the wilderness of Sinai.

One day as Moses looked for a lost sheep, he caught sight of a bush that seemed to be burning yet was not consumed; so he went closer to observe it. As he drew near, the voice of God warned him to remove his shoes because he was standing on holy ground. Then God said He had heard the cries of His people in the land of Egypt and was sending Moses to lead them out of Egypt into the land promised to their fathers.

WHO IS THE ONE TRUE GOD?

God said to Moses, "I am the God of your father, the God of Abraham, the God of Isaac, and the God of Jacob" (Exodus 3:6).

Then Moses asked God what answer he should give the Hebrews who asked for the name of the God who was sending him. God's answer was: "I AM who I AM. This is what you are to say to the Israelites: I AM has sent me to you" (v. 14).

What is this name that we translate in English with small capitals, the LORD? It stands for the Hebrew Tetragrammaton, YHWH, which is believed by scholars to be the *hiphil* tense of the Hebrew verb "to be." The translation would be, "He who causes everything to be." For reverence of the name, Orthodox Jews merely identify Him as "HaShem"—the name. But for simplicity, they took the vowel points from the word for God, "Elohim," added them to YHWH, and got "Yehowah" or Jehovah.

Jehovah had shown that He was the God who created everything that is. There was no God before Him, and there will be no God after Him. Throughout history God's name has evidenced sufficiency to His people: I am provision; I am peace; I am healing; I am victory; and in the case of Jesus, I am salvation.

Up to the time of Moses, God had revealed Himself to the patriarchs as Elohim, the Creator of the world. Only when He showed Himself as the covenant deliverer of the Jewish people did He reveal His covenant name, Jehovah.

Armed with a stick and the name of Jehovah, Moses and his brother, Aaron, went from the desert of Midian to the courts of Pharaoh, king of Egypt. In the name of Jehovah, Moses and Aaron demanded the release of the Jewish people. Pharaoh mocked the name of God in the same way people do today. "Who is Jehovah, that I should obey him and let Israel go?" he demanded (Exodus 5:2). It took ten plagues by Jehovah upon Egypt, culminating with the death of every firstborn son of the Egyptians, before Pharaoh realized that he was dealing with the most powerful deity in the universe and that it was to his advantage to do what He commanded.

Jehovah brought His chosen people out of bondage—out of Egypt—through the Sea of Reeds into Sinai, where they finally reached Mount Horeb (also called Mount Sinai).

As the Israelites gathered around the mountain, Jehovah descended in fire upon the mountaintop. This giant mountain began to shake back and forth, as with an earthquake. Thick clouds, thunder, and lightning covered the mountaintop, and the piercing blast of a ram's horn filled the air. According to the Bible, the people "trembled" (Exodus 19:16). Well, they should under those circumstances!

Jehovah warned that anyone attempting to come up the mountain would die instantly. Then at His command, Moses ascended the mountain along with his brother, Aaron.

God Himself entered into a covenant with the people. Other kings and deities had made demands of the people before, but not like this. He said, "I am Jehovah your God, who rescued you from slavery in Egypt" (Exodus 20:2 NLT). He was their deity by covenant. He was their deity by deliverance. He was the God who heard their prayers. He was the God who would go before them to lead them into the Promised Land. From the moment of their birth until their death, He would be there for them.

THE FIRST COMMANDMENT OF GOD

But the Israelites' part of the covenant was to obey ten simple rules that were put in place for their good and for the good of their society. God wrote these commandments on two stone tablets.

These Ten Commandments, and the balance of the legal code that followed it, comprised without question the most exalted legal code for human conduct in the ancient world. Nothing in the history of that time has been found to equal it. The wisdom and practicality of the Ten Commandments attest to their divine origins. As wise as Moses was, nothing in the record supports the premise that he was wise enough to draft the Mosaic Code on his own.

The Ten Commandments fit together as a unified whole. Each commandment can do much good, but the rationale for all the commandments flows from the First Commandment: "I am Jehovah your God. . . . Do not worship any other gods besides me" (Exodus 20:13, NLT).

The Christians who settled America embraced Jehovah as their God. When we say, "In God we trust," the God we mean is Jehovah God of the Ten Commandments. When we sing "God Bless America," we are singing to Jehovah God. When we swear oaths, "So help me God," we are referring to Jehovah God. When we pray, "Our Father in heaven," we are praying to Jehovah God. When Christians recite the Apostle's Creed—"I believe in God the Father, Almighty Maker of heaven and earth"—they are affirming belief in Jehovah God.

There has never been any dispute in America as to who God is. He is the God of Genesis, Exodus, the prophets, David, Jesus, and the apostles. We have had no other God throughout the history of this nation. The God who rescued the Jews from Egypt is the God of the founders of America.

So in modern times we ask ourselves, how is it possible that the acknowledgment of the same divine being throughout our history has been ruled constitutionally impermissible by one judge in Alabama?

WHO ARE THE MANY GODS?

In the book written by the prophet Isaiah, God says, "This is what Jehovah says. . . . It is I who made the earth and created mankind upon it. My own hands stretched out the heavens. I marshaled their starry hosts." "I am Jehovah, and there is no other; apart from me there is no God" (45:11–12, 5).

The First Commandment makes it clear that Jehovah will brook no rivals. Why not? First, He is the source of absolute truth, and He alone holds the key to eternal salvation. He is absolutely benevolent and totally unselfish. Since He made us, He alone knows the key to our happiness. He alone has the power to heal us, to provide for our needs, and to answer our prayers. "Other gods" are either lifeless, empty idols that are not capable of helping a human being, or these "other gods" are actually malevolent demons who will destroy their worshipers.

To see what "other gods" have done to people, it is only necessary to visit Calcutta, a city in India dedicated to Cali, the goddess of death. It was in Calcutta that Mother Teresa ministered to some of the most wretchedly poor people on the planet. This is a city where years ago the "dead truck" picked up the corpses of those who died each day from disease or starvation.

Or visit Haiti, a nation whose people prayed to Satan some 200 years ago that if he delivered them from the control of the French, they would worship him. Black magic, oppression, grinding poverty, and ceaseless killing have been the lot of the Haitians as their reward from their "other god." The island of Hispaniola is roughly divided in two. One half belongs to Haiti, which has the worst poverty in the Western Hemisphere. The other half belongs to the Dominican Republic, a prosperous and fertile land where the people worship Jehovah God. A more vivid contrast would be difficult to find.

THE BLESSINGS OF WORSHIPING GOD

Like the Dominican Republic, America has received many blessings from worshiping the one true God who has revealed Himself as supreme over all the others.

First, honoring one true God blesses us with stability as a nation, unlike those nations where warring religious factions are tearing countries apart. We should not deceive ourselves by thinking such civil unrest cannot occur here in America if the Judeo-Christian ethic that formed our stable foundation is shaken apart by the demands of competing religions.

Second, people who worship gods other than the one true God experience only spiritual confusion, uncertainty, and insecurity. Again, you have only to travel in nations where pantheons of gods demand worship and devotion in order to understand the blessing of honoring just one God.

The third great blessing in honoring the one true God is a blessing to each of us as individuals. When we worship the great I AM before all other gods, He becomes our personal source of goodness and well-being. He supplies all that we need. The Bible says that those who worship him will lack "no good thing" (Psalm 84:11).

Finally, there is another blessing that can come to each one of us as we worship the one true God. God sees in each of us the possibility of forming a new, divinely inspired nature. His Spirit helps us in our weakness to obey Him. For in fact, God's laws are a way, not to enslave us or make us jump to His service, but to form in us the good and godly character of which He knows we are capable.

To honor this God alone and follow His commands is, ultimately, to honor and respect ourselves. It is to pursue our real potential, as individuals and as a nation.

Despite these clear blessings, twenty-first-century Americans are finding the First Commandment an offense rather than a blessing. Hindus have come to this land from India, where they do not worship one god, but millions of gods according to *Hinduism Today*. They believe in a caste system where 300 million people are condemned to be lower-caste "untouchables" because of the color of their skin—cursed by Hindu belief to be born from under the foot of the god Brahma. They also worship Ganesh, a half-man, half-elephant who is a supposed son of Shiva, the god of destruction. Hindus live in great fear because they believe that after death they will be reincarnated as a cow, a snake, a dog, a dung beetle, or another person—and so on for all eternity—unless they can find cessation of desire and enter a state of existence known as Nirvana. Affirmation of faith in one God is to them seen as an offense.

Jehovah God says that each human being is a unique creation, made in His image and endowed with special rights. In the words of the Declaration of Independence, we are "created equal and endowed with inalienable rights . . . life, liberty, and the pursuit of happiness"—not fear, confusion, and grinding poverty. The concept of the exalted nature of mankind underlying all our freedoms comes only from Jehovah God of the First Commandment.

In ancient cultures, people worshiped deities such as the Egyptian sun god, Ra. A visit to the ruins of Ephesus in Turkey reveals statues of the fertility goddess Diana, portrayed as a female whose chest is covered with many breasts. The Babylonians worshiped Astarte (or Ashtoreth), who also was a fertility symbol. Usually these gods or goddesses were shown as having exaggerated genitalia, and their worship included cult prostitutes and cult sodomites. Their temples, like that at Baalbek in Lebanon, were adorned with the so-called egg and dart motif, which was a portrayal of male and female sexuality.

In ancient Canaan, people erected statues to a god called Molech. The worshipers believed that this god demanded that they sacrifice their young children to be burned alive to him. So the statue was built as a fire chamber with outstretched arms and a cavernous mouth leading to the fire chamber. Infants were placed on the statue's red-hot, outstretched arms or into the fire chamber to be burned alive.

Ancient Greece and Rome had a pantheon of gods, all of whom had human characteristics. They were capricious, vengeful, lustful, and given to quarrels among themselves. Whatever belief system that involved these gods served only to create fear, uncertainty, and lack of dignity in the minds and hearts of the worshipers.

Throughout history, human beings have worshiped the sun, the moon, the stars, animals, snakes, rulers, ancestors, Satan, and a host of representations of demonic beings which from time to time have appeared in history. The similarity of artistic representations of these terrifying demonic beings in Africa and Asia is astounding. They reflect the worldwide influence of gods, which did not come from Jehovah.

IS ALLAH THE ONE TRUE GOD?

Jehovah says that He is the one true God. Only He is the Creator. Only He is the source of wisdom. He demands that for their own good His people worship no other gods.

Today the fastest-growing religion behind Christianity is Islam. *Islam* means submission—submission to the god Allah, who was the moon god of Mecca in Saudi Arabia. This explains the presence of the crescent moon as the Islamic symbol found in the flags of many Islamic countries. Their relief agency is not the Red Cross but the Red Crescent.

I have read the writings of an expert who analyzed the origins of Middle Eastern language and population dispersal. He believes that the concept of Allah may be derived from the Canaanite and Phoenician people who inhabited the Holy Land before the Hebrews came into it from Egypt.

Whatever the origin of the name, Allah of Islam is *not* Jehovah of the First Commandment. Although Islam is a monotheistic religion, the similarity stops there. The characteristics of Jehovah and Allah are totally different.

Jehovah God revealed Himself in the Bible of the Jews and Christians, which was written by approximately forty people over a period of at least 1,400 years. In contrast, our knowledge of the god Allah comes entirely from the repetitive and internally inconsistent writing of one Arab warrior and mystic. Unlike the Koran, the Bible is internally consistent and bears clear authenticity that it was written by men who were moved upon by the Spirit of Jehovah God (2 Peter 1:20–21).

Many people, including some Christians, think that Jehovah God and Allah are the same. They are not! Anyone who equates Jehovah God with Allah of the Koran is committing a grave historical, and equally grave theological, error.

Obviously, since the First Commandment forbids the worship of "other gods" such as Allah, this commandment meant for our good is seen as an offense to Muslims, who of necessity wish it removed from public view.

New Age Gods Abound

America is also being overtaken with various forms of New Age belief. Some worship Gaia, the "great mother," calling upon the ancient energies of the earth contained in the elements of earth, air, fire, and water. Others worship the "sky father," who is consort to the "great mother" and coequal to her. Still others worship "Sophia," the feminine embodiment of secret wisdom.

"White witchcraft" in America has transformed from a collection of games played at teen slumber parties to a religion gaining status and rights. Wicca, as it is known, boasts thousands of covens and "churches" dedicated to "the old ways." These covens do not meet down dark alleys or in forsaken cemeteries at night. Many are registered with the government as tax-exempt religious organizations and can be found in our towns and cities, or tucked in among farmlands in the heart of our nation. On one such farm in rural southeastern Pennsylvania, pagans of various stripes from druids to witches meet annually to help raise a circle of standing stones, before which they make offerings on a stone altar to their gods and to the "powers" within the stones themselves.

Then comes the train of "nature deities." Many of the deities to whom Americans are turning are the old gods of Celtic myth and legend. We have turned to the worship of the so-called ancient energies of the earth and the cosmos, despite the biblical warning to resist powers and principalities, which are really demonic entities that rule in high places and war against the one true God. New Agers seek out various types of mediums and astrologers, hoping to hear cosmic wisdom either channeled to them from spirits or written in the stars. Millions and millions more Americans, some of whom are even churchgoing people, are dabbling in magic and seeking occasional guidance from tarot cards, Ouija boards, and daily horoscopes.

We are even experiencing a small revival of Roman and Greek paganism, as some return to the mystery religions of ancient Rome and Greece. We are going back to the worship of gods who are just like humans, with their fickle natures, their deceits and lust, and their cowardliness and murdering ways.

It is time we stopped to ask: How is it that, in this complex technological age, we have returned to the worship of gods from whom our ancestors fought to free themselves? Why have we returned to gods of fear and darkness and elevated to the status of deities such things as trees, stones, and crawling creatures?

MAN AS HIS OWN GOD

On the surface, it seems that America has become a nation that runs after many other gods. But the truth is, in America we worship ourselves. To worship something means to hold it in high esteem, to respect it as sacred. If we were truly a people who worshiped God, we would hold Him and His commandments in a place higher than ourselves. But that is often not the case. For some time, a major shift has been taking place in our culture. Where we once worshiped and held in high esteem the God of the Bible and His laws, we now worship another god—that is, the individual. We worship us.

The supreme love of self has been ongoing in America ever since the Enlightenment of the eighteenth century began to run counter to the great spiritual awakenings of that era. While Enlightenment thinking gave birth to many wonderful scientific, educational, and artistic movements, latent in it was the metaphysical concept that the highest and ultimate authority is not God, but the individual.

Late in the 1800s, individualism subtly began to take the form of a secular religion. It was then that the poet Walt Whitman gave a popular voice to this religion when he wrote in his introduction to *Leaves of Grass:* "There will soon be no more priests. Their work is done ... every man shall be his own priest." Whitman was only one voice, trumpeting the tenet that America's cultural elitists readily adopted. To reverence and obey anything or anyone above our intellect, our passions, and ourselves became a ridiculous notion.

It is not surprising that the Enlightenment also brought a landslide of scholarship aimed at destroying our respect for the authority of the Bible. By the late 1800s, what had become known as higher criticism had pressed the Bible firmly under the heel of man. Rather than allowing the Word of God to direct people's behavior and affairs, intellectuals placed themselves and their reasoning above the Bible. The ongoing autopsy of the Bible, which they began, continues to this day. Higher criticism, for its claim that it seeks the truth, really begins with the notion that Scripture is man-made and not God-inspired. Therefore, these critics hold that the Bible is gravely flawed and untrustworthy. It is then up to these critics to "correct" mistaken ideas created by this "flawed" Bible.

THE GODS OF PSYCHOLOGY

From the early part of the twentieth century, the development of psychological sciences hastened the erosion of our nation's early stance that there is one true God who is supreme and to be obeyed. From Sigmund Freud and Carl Jung came the idea that there is a great subconscious that powerfully governs our actions and our lives. As psychology and spirituality crossed paths, the powers of the human soul became God. Subsequent theorists in the field of myth and depth psychology, such as Joseph Campbell and James Hillman, have continued to strengthen the belief that we do not realize our greatest good by obeying God and His laws. Instead, our greatest good comes as each one of us follows our individual "bliss" and emerges as a self-actualized individual, free from any "laws" we do not accept. To those who promote such radical individuation, any standard that asks us to conform to laws apart from those we create for ourselves is repressive and evil.

The effect of all these movements is that the spirit of America has been turned upside-down. Today, our culture mocks anyone who insists that we return to the worship of the one true God. We especially demonize anyone who insists that His laws must be obeyed. Through despising the worship of the one true God and His laws, we have created a secular religion—the cult of the individual.

While there are many negative consequences spawned by the cult of the individual, perhaps the most widespread is this: As a culture, we hold little respect for any position of authority. We hate laws that "limit" our behavior. No longer do we honor people for the positions they hold—not parents, teachers, employers, officers of the law, or government officials. Our lack of respect has reached mammoth proportions. As this social illness deepens, our nation is hurtling toward devastating social and personal consequences. Even in the church, we are losing our respect for our ministers, elders, and teachers, and uprisings against pastors and church leaders are epidemic.

As a result of our great disregard for authority, it grates on us to hear: "I am the LORD your God. . . . Do not worship any other gods besides me." It has become offensive to say that there is one God who claims to be supreme and who calls for our obedience.

Why are we so offended? Because we do not like the truth that there is One who is above us because He is the Supreme Being, the Creator of the universe. We do not like the fact that He alone has absolute power and wisdom or that the laws by which He holds all things together are absolute and unchanging, just like His moral laws.

SEDUCTIVE CONTEMPORARY GODS

If we are going to point out those who have turned from the God of the Bible to foreign religions, we must also consider those who have made "gods" out of various aspects of our materialistic culture.

To many American businessmen, capitalism has the stature of a god. The worship of capitalism allows men and women like the heads of Enron and WorldCom to say, "We're the ones who make this country run. We create jobs and make the economy work. Therefore, if it's good for us, it will be good for everyone." Because these people believe in capitalism above all, they believe they can decide what is right and wrong. The result is deception and economic disaster.

In the educational community, we honor the human mind above God. The concept of revelation from outside ourselves is considered not only antiquated, but nonsense. Anyone who relies on truth from above is regarded as dangerous and possibly insane.

In the medical community, we see doctors who venerate biotechnology. Here in Norfolk, Virginia, doctors are playing God by creating life in a Petri dish. We are just steps away from the work of the doctors in China who recently cloned a life form that is a cross between an animal and a human to harvest stem cells. Science has become a law unto itself, and the rule is: If we can do it, it should be allowed.

On the everyday level, Americans have sacrificed greatly to the gods of materialism. We give up our days for more money—in some cases working up to sixty, eighty, and one hundred twenty hours a week. We ignore our spiritual lives and run ourselves to emptiness, weariness, and depletion. Then we sink into depression. As a result, we have a nationwide epidemic of overmedicated people.

THE SENSUAL GODS OF POP CULTURE

Even our pop culture has given us gods: professional athletes, movie stars, fashion models, and recording artists. These are the people to whom we look, emulating these celebrities and their life-styles. Oddly enough, many of these people experience tragedy because of their wild lifestyles and character flaws. Still, millions continue to follow them.

Interestingly, the worshipers of these false gods all suffer from a kind of spiritual blindness. They apparently do not see the one characteristic shared by every idol and false god: Not one of them is supreme.

Whether we are speaking of Buddha or Allah or nature deities, the powers false gods claim come from some aspect of creation—for instance, its cyclical nature, its fertility, or its destructiveness. If we look closely, we see that none of these false gods has any power over creation. Yet practitioners of religions that worship these gods do not seem to stop and ask themselves, "How can my god be God if he is subject to the conditions of creation?" Quite simply, these so-called gods cannot be free from the bounds of the created universe.

There is another truth that millions are not willing to face. The false gods we turn to are in many ways suspiciously like us. Is this a coincidence? That's doubtful. What is far more likely is that we have projected ourselves large onto the broad screen of the cosmos and called it "god." Among America's false gods, besides the idols imported from other cultures, we have created our own pantheon. We worship our own desire for comfort and luxury through our materialism. We worship our overblown sense of intelligence through our intellectualism. We worship our bodies and our senses through our sensationalism. In short, we have taken what is weak and low in human nature and elevated it to the status of the good and the holy.

What, you may ask, is the problem with that? What is wrong with elevating the good in humankind and honoring that which is highest and best in us? And isn't a lack of respect for nature the reason we are destroying the environment and our own planet? What is wrong with the worship of idols and false gods?

TOLERANCE BECOMES ITS OWN GOD

Anyone who speaks against the worship of other gods besides Jehovah, the God of the Bible, is going to rankle his fellow Americans. We are a nation that prizes religious tolerance. In fact, *tolerance* has become one of the most popular words in our culture. We believe, as a nation where free speech and the right of expression prevail, that every viewpoint and belief should be represented without hindrance.

On the surface, tolerance is indeed a good social stance. We do not want America to become a nation where minority opinions and beliefs are repressed, or where individuals are brutalized for beliefs that run counter to the mainstream. Some of our great cultural heroes are those who stood against mainstream thinking and suffered the intolerance of mobs in order to bring about social change.

But tolerance has an extremely unhealthy aspect as well. What we have meant by "tolerance" is a weakening of the lines between good and evil, right and wrong.

A pagan religious group that worships nature deities with exaggerated genitalia wants tolerance for its rituals—even though they include worship in the nude with groups that include children and culminate in men and women worshiping their gods through open sexual intercourse.

Groups claiming the most tenuous relationship to Native American religion demand tolerance for their practices, which include the use of dangerous, mind-altering, illegal drugs.

Certain fundamentalist sects, rooted in Middle Eastern religions, demand that we tolerate their hate-filled rhetoric, aimed at destroying "America, the great Satan."

In our culture as a whole, the false gods of our right to free speech and expression have blurred the lines, particularly between decency and pornography. As I write, the advertising trailer for *Coupling*—one of the new (and thankfully short-lived) television offerings on NBC—features all six main characters seemingly in the nude.

What is wrong with the worship of false gods? They do not speak with a voice of authority, declaring what is good and what is evil, right and wrong. Suspiciously, they speak in permissive terms, granting us leave to do that which appeals to our flesh and to the darker impulses in our souls—for revenge and the fulfillment of our lusts. They motivate us to sink to the level of predators bent on consuming each other.

MODERN SELF-HELP DEITIES

It is no wonder we have tolerated the rise of false gods in America. We have only to peruse the "self-help" and "spirituality" titles in any bookstores, and there we will find evidence of the single most prominent god in our culture.

One of the most popular self-help gurus of recent years is Thomas Moore, a Catholic monk turned depth psychologist. In Moore's first bestseller, *Care of the Soul,* he helps us understand why God's laws and His prohibition against false idols is an offense today. He writes, "Care of the soul is in many ways a return to early notions of what therapy is. *Cura,* the Latin word used originally in 'care of the soul,' means several things: attention, devotion, husbandry, healing, managing, being anxious for, and worshiping the gods." He further writes, "I do not use the word [soul] here as an object of religious belief or as something to do with immorality. . . . I see my responsibility, to myself, to a friend, or to a patient in therapy, as observing and respecting what the soul presents."

In fact, what Moore is suggesting is "attention" and "devotion" to "the gods" represented by the various moods, likes, and loves of the soul itself. Throughout the rest of his book, Moore helps the reader to identify with the desires and exploits of various pagan gods and to "honor" them. To Moore, "worshiping" or "honoring" the gods and our desires means to place the likes and wants of our own multifaceted soul above all. To him, and to other depth psychologists who employ his methods on a wide scale, the human soul is apparently the supreme force, a collection of hungry deities. Every wish, desire, and fantasy is a god to be served. If we want to be blissful and fulfilled, we should lavish attention upon these gods of our every whim.

In a culture where tolerance is the highest good and where each individual soul has become a false god to be honored and served, it is a grievous offense for the God of the Bible to declare, "Do not worship any other gods besides me."

The question for us as individuals and as a nation is simple: Will we serve ourselves, or will we make God the Lord of our lives? A nation that serves millions and millions of individual, small "gods" all bent on having their own way will not stand. But a nation that worships the one true God will be unified, strong, and secure. For then and only then will God prove Himself to be the great I AM, capable of meeting our every need.

FIVE

Commandment Two: Avoid Worshiping Idols

Do not make idols of any kind. . . .
You must never worship or bow down to them.

—EXODUS 20:4–5 NLT

SEVERAL YEARS AGO I was in Rajahmundry, India, to speak at a conference and shoot a television documentary. Early one morning my camera crew and I went to the side of the river that flowed through the city of Rajahmundry. The native people believed that the river contained the sperm of the god Shiva, so they came early in the morning to dip themselves in what they considered to be a supernatural elixir. All around the steps leading down to the river were statues of their gods and goddesses. The ominous statue of Shiva, the god who is believed to destroy and then rebuild, was set apart from the other idols. Shiva was portrayed sitting cross-legged, staring into space. Two cobras were wrapped around his neck, turned toward each side of his face, supposedly giving him wisdom.

Around the patio leading to the river I observed Indian men and women bowing with their faces on the ground before stone statues of various gods, begging them for answers to their prayers. I thought, *Don't these people realize that these lifeless hunks of rock can't help them?* Yet there they were, offering sacrifices and prayers to that which had no ears and could not speak.

I also witnessed this kind of devotion to idols when I visited a Buddhist temple in Taipei in the 1980s. I watched as worshipers would buy little slips of paper from vendors along the wall. They would then bow down and pray to a giant statue of Buddha while they burned incense—even money—in the hopes that the fortune expressed in the little slip of paper would favor them. Some had special fortune sticks that they threw on the ground in front of the statue in hopes of learning some secret of the future.

Imagine the heartaches, disappointments, and wasted dreams of those who invest their hopes in an idol that can do them no good.

THE FOOLISHNESS OF IDOL WORSHIP

The Second Commandment is explicit: *"Do not make idols of any kind,* whether in the shape of birds or animals or fish. You must never worship or bow down to them" (Exodus 20:4–5 NLT; emphasis added).

The prophet Isaiah mocked those in Israel who violated God's commandment and venerated idols. Here are his words:

Then the wood-carver measures and marks out a block of wood, takes the tool, and carves the figure of a man. Now he has a wonderful idol that cannot even move from where it is placed! . . . He plants the cedar in the forest. . . . And after his care, he uses part of the wood to make a fire to warm himself and bake his bread. Then—yes, it's true—he takes the rest of it and makes himself a god for people to worship! He makes an idol and bows down and praises it! He burns part of the tree to roast his meat and to keep himself warm. Then he takes what's left and makes his god: a carved idol! He falls down in front of it, worshiping and praying to it. "Rescue me!" he says. "You are my god!"

Such stupidity and ignorance! Their eyes are closed, and they cannot see. Their minds are shut, and they cannot think. The person who made the idol never stops to reflect. . . . The poor, deluded fool feeds on ashes. He is trusting something that can give him no help at all. Yet he cannot bring himself to ask, "Is this thing, this idol that I'm holding in my hand, a lie?" (Isaiah 44:13–20 NLT)

There was once a time when Americans agreed with Isaiah that the worship of idols is utterly foolish and springs from paganism. Jehovah's revelation expressed in the Jewish and Christian religion is infinitely superior to paganism. Yet in the climate of political correctness that has now descended like a shroud over America's liberal elite, any attempt to show the superiority of one religion over another is met with derision and hostility. In fact, at the United Nations repeated attempts have been made to criminalize the conversion of idol worshipers to the truth.

Having successfully muzzled the truth in our universities and the media, the high priests and high priestesses of political correctness have opened the doors in once-Christian America to the onslaught and veneration of Hindu deities, Buddhist monks, Indian shamans, Satanism, black magic, and occultism. Those who protest are labeled right-wing, fundamentalist, narrow-minded bigots. It is now considered un-American to criticize anyone's religion, except Christianity.

Yet the truth cannot be muzzled. I once heard of a wonderful story out of Africa. In a remote village in deepest Africa lived a man who made a living carving and selling idols. One day the light went on inside his being. He looked at his arm that held the chisel and his other arm, which held the idol, and he thought, *If my arm can carve this idol, I must worship the One who made my arm.* So he set himself to pray to discover the Creator of his arm. Obviously, the God who sees, hears, and performs miracles did not wait long to answer. He blessed this African carver of idols with a revelation of Himself, and the carver became a fervent believer in the God who made his arm and who sent His Son to die for his sins.

THE DIFFERENCE BETWEEN GOD AND IDOLS

Why is idolatry so easy and worship of the one true God so difficult?

We are spiritual beings, but our spirits are housed in a finite body. We are surrounded by things that stimulate our physical senses. We feel comfortable around objects that we can see, touch, taste, or feel. Most people are intensely uncomfortable around ethereal beings that have no defined body. The scary part of horror movies comes from the introduction of the ghostly wraith that belongs to some reality other than what our physical senses can perceive.

Yet Jehovah God introduced Himself as pure being. He is life itself. He controls electricity and atomic power. He is the energy source for the sun and the stars. Jesus Christ said, "God is spirit, and his worshipers must worship in spirit and in truth" (John 4:24).

The problem with this for the average person is that in order to commune with God, the worshiper must be holy. The Psalmist wrote, "Who may ascend the hill of Jehovah? Who may stand in his holy place? He who has clean hands and a pure heart, who does not lift up his soul to an idol" (Psalm 24:3–4). God has said that His people are to be holy, for He is holy (1 Peter 1:16).

A God like this is always lifting people higher and higher in purity, morality, kindness to others, surrender of self, and love. When we worship Jehovah God, we are purified and refined . . . made increasingly like Him.

But people desire something concrete, not spiritual. They want to see a statue of a deity, an image of a saint, or a representation of someone who can bring good fortune and help ease life's burdens. They can rub the idol, touch the idol, kiss the idol, and bow down before the idol without any reformation of life whatsoever. The idol becomes whatever the worshiper desires. Yet the idol can never give peace, can never answer the longings of the heart, can never forecast the future, and certainly can never lead a worshiper to true holiness. Religion based on idols will lead either to degeneracy or to painful asceticism. Idolatry always leads to disappointment and frustration.

DEMONIC INFLUENCE OF IDOLS

In this world there are beings that are not human. The Bible speaks of spiritual beings called angels, who are the messengers of God. These beings are sent to announce important events to mankind, but, more significantly, they are sent by God to watch over the human beings called the "heirs of salvation" (Hebrews 1:14 KJV). The popularity of the weekly television series *Touched by an Angel,* plus the numerous books on the subject, bear witness to the fact that a substantial majority of Americans believe in angels.

However, the Bible tells us that one-third of the angels joined Lucifer, also known as Satan, in a revolt against Jehovah God (see Revelation 12:4, 9). These angels in rebellion are called demons, and God has confined them to planet earth. Satan and the demons fight God and, in turn, despise human beings who are made in God's image.

Demons yearn to receive the homage and worship due Jehovah God. Their goal is to frustrate God's desire to bring people to heaven; to debase people in every way possible, especially as it concerns human reproduction; and ultimately to take people to hell. In the process, demons yearn to receive the worship due God. Demons want human beings to sacrifice to them and to worship and adore them.

Therefore, it is not uncommon in societies where idol worship is prevalent to realize that the inanimate statues, amulets, and charms actually are the homes of demonic beings reveling in the worship given to them through the idol.

Jehovah God understood all too well the evil schemes of his enemy and his enemy's minions. One of the blessings of the Second Commandment is that it protects God's people from mortal danger.

MORAL CONSEQUENCES OF IDOLATRY

Yet in a world where polytheism and idolatry are more and more common, it is easy to see that a commandment from a loving God meant to keep people from danger can become an offense. The apostle Paul in his letter to the church at Rome laid out in vivid detail how each stage of spiritual apostasy can lead to the next. Here is a description of the decline of first-century religious belief that parallels precisely what is happening in twenty-first-century Europe and America:

> Yes, they knew God, but they wouldn't worship Him as God or even give Him thanks. And they began to think up foolish ideas of what God was like. The result was that their minds became dark and confused. Claiming to be wise, they became utter fools instead. And instead of worshiping the glorious, ever-living God, they worshiped idols made to look like mere people, or birds and animals and snakes.

> So God let them go ahead and do whatever shameful things their hearts desired. As a result, they did vile and degrading things with each other's bodies. Instead of believing what they knew was the truth about God, they deliberately chose to believe lies. So they worshiped the things God made, but not the Creator himself, who is to be praised forever. Amen.

> That is why God abandoned them to their shameful desires. Even the women turned against the natural way to have sex and instead indulged in sex with each other. And the men, instead of having normal sexual relationships with women,

burned with lust for each other. Men did shameful things with other men and, as a result, suffered within themselves the penalty they so richly deserved.

When they refused to acknowledge God, he abandoned them to their evil minds. . . . Their lives became full of every kind of wickedness, sin, greed, hate, envy, murder, fighting, deception, malicious behavior, and gossip. . . . They are fully aware of God's death penalty for those who do these things, yet they go right ahead and do them anyway. And, worse yet, they encourage others to do them, too. (Romans 1:21–32 NLT)

Paul wrote of people doing vile and degrading things with one another's bodies. Can anyone conceive of anything more vile than the taxpayer-funded exhibit of photographs by Robert Mapplethorpe, which prominently featured a naked man with a bull whip protruding from his rectum—or the taxpayer-supported stage production of a naked woman covered in chocolate meant to simulate feces? Indeed, the ultimate end of the idolatry that arises from the worship of man, his science, his intellect, his philosophy, and his scorn of his Creator will lead to a short circuit in the process of human reproduction and to vile sexual excesses, both heterosexual and homosexual.

At one time we shunned these sexual practices—we were revolted by them and even criminalized them. In 2003, the darkened minds of a majority of Supreme Court judges reversed 200 years of Christian belief and declared sodomy to be a constitutional right. In Canada, the situation is worse. In that country fines and criminal penalties attach to anyone who speaks out against sexual perversion and calls it sin.

The Bible makes it clear that the widespread acceptance of idolatry and sexual perversion in a society is clear evidence that God has "abandoned them." There is a yawning chasm developing in our nation between evangelical Christian standards of morality and the morality of the general public.

A Barna Research poll released on November 3, 2003, chronicles the alarming decay of American moral standards. According to Barna, of ten moral behaviors evaluated, 61 percent of Americans believe that gambling is "morally acceptable," 60 percent believe cohabitation without marriage is morally acceptable, and 59 percent say the same about sexual fantasies (including, I presume, cybersex and phone sex). Abortion was considered morally acceptable by 45 percent of Americans, and 42 percent considered it morally acceptable to have sexual relations with someone of the opposite sex other than their spouse. Well over one-third considered pornography, profanity, and drunkenness morally acceptable, and 30 percent felt the same way about homosexual sex.

Barna believes that his findings show in only two years a marked jump in acceptance by the general population of activities and lifestyles that were once considered immoral or sinful. According to Barna:

> Most of the people we interviewed believe that they are highly moral individuals and identify other people as responsible for the nation's moral decline. This is reflective of a nation where morality is generally defined according to one's feelings. In a postmodern society, where people do not acknowledge any moral absolutes, if a person feels justified in engaging in a special behavior, then they do not make a connection with the immoral nature of that action. Yet deep inside they sense that something is wrong in our society.
>
> Until people recognize that there are moral absolutes and attempt to live in harmony with them, we are likely to see a continued decay of our moral foundations. . . . The generational data patterns made a compelling case for this ongoing

slide. Even most people associated with the Christian faith do not seem to have embraced biblical moral standards.

GOD—ABOVE ALL THINGS

This moral decline about which Barna reports is especially alarming given the most compelling reason worshiping idols and false gods is so destructive. The God who gave us the commandment to not worship idols is not part of the created universe. He is transcendent, existing above and apart from His creation. He is the only being who is not subject to the conditions and laws of nature. False gods are themselves subject to the creation. They have no power and cannot be trusted to direct our personal pathways. Only the God of the Bible, who is above all things, can produce miracles. And only he can direct us, by His Holy Spirit, guiding us into the lives of purpose and meaning for which we long.

At the same time, this almighty God who rules over all is the one who declares that He loves us and commits Himself to us "with an everlasting covenant" (Isaiah 55:3; Ezekiel 16:60). He is the only God who has ever bound himself to mankind in this irrevocable way. And in Jesus Christ, He has offered us the opportunity to know Him personally and to fellowship with Him continuously. With this great revelation of a personal God, millions of believers have found a deep security because we know that no matter what happens to us in this world, our soul's safety is firm in Him.

And so, worshiping the one true God alone, we have something our souls deeply crave—that is, freedom from the terrible isolation and emptiness that gnaw at the soul of every one of us. He fills the "God-shaped vacuum" in every heart that opens to Him. When we worship the true God, we experience intimate fellowship with the One who will never leave us or forsake us (Hebrews 13:5). What greater blessing can there be than this?

A LIGHT ON THE HORIZON

But while formerly Christian America is seemingly turning its back on these extraordinary blessings and embracing idols and false doctrines, an amazing phenomenon is taking place in what used to be called the Third World but is now known as the Global South. In these nations, Christianity is booming. The Christianity in these lands is Bible-based, evangelical, and, in large part, charismatic. There are now many more Anglicans in Nigeria than there are in Great Britain—many more Presbyterians in Ghana than in Scotland.

Recently, the Episcopal Church in the United States ordained as bishop Gene Robinson, who since his divorce from his wife has taken up with a homosexual lover. The world Anglican Communion counts 77 million members, the Episcopal Church USA about 2.3 million members. The prelates of African and Asian churches exploded in wrath at the clear departure of the Episcopal Church into heresy and apostasy. These huge bodies of believers have not been contaminated with situational ethics or political correctness. Homosexuality and adultery to them are clearly wrong, and they will have nothing to do with such practices.

While it seems that God is surrendering the United States and Europe to "shameful desires," His truth is spreading like wildfire in those countries once gripped by idolatry. Christianity is the world's fastest-growing religion and is on the way to three billion adherents worldwide. Only in societies where the cultural elites have deliberately suppressed the excellence of the Christian gospel to transform lives has Christianity failed to have explosive growth.

Consider China, which, with 1.2 billion inhabitants, is the world's largest nation. From its founding until the Chin dynasty in approximately 200 BC, China practiced a pure monotheism that paralleled precisely the monotheism of the Old Testament. The God of China is called Shanti (or Shandi). His attributes are similar to the Jehovah God of the Law of Moses.

During the Shia dynasty (or Tsia dynasty), some 2,200 years before Christ, the emperor of China entered what we know as Tiananmen Square to ascend the steps of the Temple of Heaven to offer elaborate sacrifices to Shanti. In this ceremony, known as the Border Sacrifice, the emperor of China prostrated himself before the God of heaven to acknowledge that he ruled all of China only as a servant of the one true God, Shanti.

Inside the Temple of Heaven was a throne—but on it was no statue, no idol. Instead, placed on the throne was a placard bearing the name *Shanti.* The God of China had shown the Chinese what He had shown Moses: that His power is so great and His being so awesome that no possible representation was suitable to portray Him. God revealed Himself as "I AM that I AM" to the Hebrews and "Shanti, the Lord of Heaven" to the Chinese.

Now the God of heaven is bringing China back to Himself. There are between eighty million to one hundred million Christians in China today. Expert observers like former *Time* magazine Beijing bureau chief David Aikman see a time in the not-too-distant future when 20 to 30 percent of the Chinese population will be Christian. If and when that happens, China will emerge as the foremost Christian nation on earth. Without idols, without a corrosive belief system, China will experience God's overwhelming blessing of being free to worship Him according to the truth of the Bible and free to take the knowledge of the one true God across Asia and the Middle East, as they say, "Back to Jerusalem."

The world is moving toward a time when the one true God is worshiped and His commandments are considered a blessing, not an offense. May our great nation not be left behind as this miracle unfolds!

Six

Commandment Three: Honor God's Name

Do not misuse the name of Jehovah your God.
Jehovah will not let you go unpunished if you misuse his name.

—Exodus 20:7 NLT

As we have seen, the name of Jehovah describes His very existence as the One who caused everything in the universe to be. God's name makes known His person and His glory. If His name is misused, then the person so doing is despising not just a name, but God Himself.

What does it mean to misuse God's name? First of all, the Hebrew text does not support the premise that people are forbidden to utter the name of God. We can use His name in prayer, we can sing songs to Him, and we can mention His greatness. Obviously, the discussion of His name in the pages of this book does not violate any commandment. Hopefully, this book will serve to honor and glorify God.

Misuse of the name of Jehovah includes employing His name for empty, vain, and unworthy objects. Further explanation of this commandment is found in the book of Leviticus, where the commandment is stated, "Do not use my name to swear a falsehood and so profane the name of your God" (Leviticus 19:12 NLT)

Jesus Christ ordered His disciples not to swear by the temple, or by the gold in the temple, or by heaven because it is the throne of

God, and, of course, never by the name of Jehovah. He said, "Let your 'Yes' be 'Yes' and your 'No,' 'No'; anything beyond this comes from the evil one" (Matthew 5:37). Interestingly, our official oaths come close to breaking this commandment, but they end in a prayer, "So help me God," not an oath that says, "By God I swear it."

So the Third Commandment forbids us to associate God's name with that which is empty, vain, false, and for which there is no occasion. Obviously, the commandment forbids trivial swearing in the normal course of daily life.

Breaking this commandment should never be taken lightly, for Jehovah God says He "will not hold him guiltless"—this means unpunished—who takes His name in vain (Exodus 20:7 KJV). To put it another way, Jehovah God has promised that He will guarantee punishment to every individual who violates this commandment.

How then does the Third Commandment play out in the day-to-day life of a nation, its citizens, and that smaller group of people who claim to belong to Jehovah God?

USING GOD'S NAME "IN VAIN"

"You *have* to go see this film," friends insisted. "There's no doubt *Seabiscuit* is going to be nominated for Best Film at the Academy Awards this year."

With that strong endorsement from people whose opinion I valued, I went to see the film. And when I filed out of the packed theater a little more than two hours later, I agreed with my friends' assessment. The dynamic footage of the horse races was amazing. You could almost feel the dirt flying up from the horses' thundering hooves and the crush of the rival horses' flanks as the jockeys fought to edge each other out. And what could be more moving than the story of Americans down on their luck but making a comeback to triumph over all odds?

Yet one aspect of the film bothered me. One of the main characters slung around the name of God when he was angry like so much muck and manure from a horse's stall. On his lips, the name of God was reduced to nothing more than a gross profanity.

I realize as I voice these thoughts that American pop culture has been hard at work for a long time pushing the boundaries of decency. I realize that strings of four-letter words are commonplace in our music, films, plays, and books today. I realize that God Himself has been "interpreted" in unflattering ways—depicted as morally ambiguous by Alanis Morrissette, as a doddering old jokester by George Burns, and as the sex partner of Mary Magdalene by Willem Dafoe.

I realized that day, leaving the film *Seabiscuit,* that in our culture using the name of God as a curse is, comparatively, nothing. No big deal. And that is exactly my point.

In America, using the name of God "in vain" (as the King James Version puts it) means little or nothing to most of us. We do it all the time, not just to vent our anger and frustration, but in various other ways as well. And when we're confronted about profaning God's name, we take offense.

A secretary complains to her boss that she is bothered by other managers' use of the name Jesus Christ as a curse because she is a Christian. She tells him that hearing him use the words "God" and "damn" together also troubles her. In a month she's replaced and told it's because she has a problem getting along with coworkers and does not fit in. Her boss tells her, "Look, if you want to get along in the business world, you can't wear your religion on your sleeve."

A Christian businessman confronts his partner, a nonbeliever, about lies he's told. "And the ugly part of it is, you told me a lie and said, 'I swear to God this is true.'" His partner sneers disgustedly. "What is this—Sunday school? I resent you implying I'm some kind of sinner!"

USING GOD'S NAME TO CURSE OTHERS

Why is God's prohibition against using His name in vain such an offense to people?

For most Americans, "misusing" the name of God merely means saying the word "God" and following it with a condemning word. In anger, we damn someone and ask God's help in doing so. When this sentiment is directed at us, we feel shocked, offended, or angry.

In the New Testament, Jesus said, "You have heard that it was said to the people long ago, 'Do not murder, and anyone who murders will be subject to judgment.' But I tell you . . . anyone who says to his brother, 'Raca,' is answerable to the Sanhedrin" (Matthew 5:21–22).

"Raca" is an Aramaic term of contempt. To tell someone they are "raca" means you have judged them as worthless, like trash, to be discarded or thrown out. Jesus makes it clear that condemning someone else places us in danger of judgment ourselves. It is not our place to judge the worth of another human being, and most assuredly not our place to condemn anyone's soul.

Yet it offends many Americans to be confronted about their casual cursing of others in God's name. Ours is a God with whom people do not like to deal, because His very name calls them to account for the wrong they have done and the good they have failed to do. People do not like to have their consciences stirred. If you confront people about using the name of Jesus as an expletive, they will likely consider you "a religious fanatic" or "one of those holier-than-thou Christians."

At the root of their offense lies this fact: Americans do not like to have anyone point out their lack of self-control as they vent their anger, jealousy, or frustration in ugly and inappropriate ways. They resent having their consciences stirred by someone who holds a greater respect for God and for His Son.

USING GOD'S NAME FOR PERSONAL GAIN

There is another reason that this prohibition against misusing God's name offends our culture. For some of us, invoking God has become a powerful tool we use to get things we want.

A businessman loads on the Christian-sounding lingo when he wants to impress potential clients and get their business.

A woman insists, "God told me to . . ." every time she wants to justify her own preferences and decisions.

A politician laces a few biblical quotations through his speeches to court the conservative Christian vote when he, himself, has no real interest in honoring God.

As a result of this kind of manipulation, unsuspecting people let down their guard. Sometimes the results are disastrous.

When Dan and Marilyn decided to have the basement of their home turned into a family area and guest room, Dan invited several small contractors to look over their plans, take measurements, and give estimates. When the bids were in, it came down to two men. The standout was the one whose speech and manners made it obvious he was a Christian.

Dan and Marilyn made the decision to hire Jerry when he delivered the bid to them in person one evening. Just before leaving, he asked if they could pray together. "Father," Jerry began, "whoever Dan and Marilyn hire to work on their home, let this building project be a blessing." And as he left, he added, "You know how things can go wrong when you're under construction. I'd just hate to see you two get hooked up with someone who wouldn't watch out for your best interests and treat you right."

Even though Jerry's was not the lowest bid, that evidence of personal care impressed Dan and Marilyn. Jerry got the job.

By the time the project was over, however, Dan and Marilyn had gone through a nightmare. Jerry began the job all right, but two weeks into it, he started vanishing on and off, sometimes for more than a week at a time while their project stalled. Dan's work demanded that he travel frequently, so Marilyn was left to phone and phone and phone. For days her calls would go unanswered; then Jerry would suddenly show up without apology or explanation, work for a day or two, and then vanish again.

To make things worse, when Dan came home from one long trip, he inspected the work and found it to be appallingly substandard. The framing was shoddy and the dry wall uneven. When Dan called Jerry over to show him the problems, Jerry tried to turn the tables. "I should have known you people expected too much. You told me you were concerned about keeping the costs down, and so I bid this job low—real low—to help you out. I don't want to be rude or anything, but you left a woman in charge of the job, so when I have questions, there's really nobody to ask.

"Frankly," Jerry finished, "I'm the one who should be complaining. I'm losing money here."

When Dan stood his ground and insisted Jerry redo the poor work, Jerry began shouting and cursing. Then he walked out, slamming the door behind him. Even worse, when Dan checked the building account, he found it was nearly empty, even though the work was barely half-done. Jerry had talked Marilyn into advancing him several thousand dollars from the account, even though no draw was due. "Because I thought he was a believer," Marilyn said angrily, "I trusted him when he said he needed the money, even though he was asking for it ahead of schedule."

The sad truth about what happened to Dan and Marilyn is that Jerry used the name of God, filling his conversations with talk about "the Lord Jesus" and making a pretense at being a devout Christian, just to gain their confidence. On his lips, the words "God" and the name "Jesus Christ" were nothing more than pure manipulation, bait to draw in the innocent and unsuspecting.

A few years ago there was a catchy pop song called "Games People Play." One of the lines says it all: "In the name of the Lord, they sock it to you, games people play." Far too many are "socking it to" the unsuspecting in the name of the Lord. They peddle phony investment schemes, phony insurance policies, phony real estate, phony tax shelters, phony retirement communities, phony pyramid schemes, and phony computer-generated arbitrage—all in the name of the Lord and usually to their coreligionists.

The kind of people who use the name of God for their own selfish gain are under God's wrath. To them, the Third Commandment is an offense. "You shall not misuse the name of the LORD" (Exodus 20:7).

USING GOD'S NAME WHILE DISHONORING HIM

There is an even greater crime against people than manipulating them to get their favorable opinion, their vote, or their money. It is the crime of misusing the name of God in a way that seriously damages or potentially destroys their souls.

Those of us who claim to be Christians are declaring to the world that we are the living representatives of God Most High and of His Son, Jesus Christ. When we blaspheme the name of God by the way we live, we are misusing the name of God. Of course, we all fail to honor God from time to time. I am referring here to people whose lifestyle continually contradicts the character of the God they claim to serve.

We break the Third Commandment by saying we are Christians while choosing to live habitually in ways that dishonor God and go against His Holy Word. As Paul wrote with great sadness to the Jews of his day, "You who brag about the law, do you dishonor God by breaking the law? As it is written, 'God's name is blasphemed among the Gentiles because of you'" (Romans 2:23–24). While the Jews of Paul's day insisted they were God's chosen people, protectors of the true faith, and keepers of His Law, they themselves found innumerable ways around the Law. They had become blind to their own sins and failures because they were so hard at work pointing out where everyone else was sinning.

I believe we need to look at parallels between what these so-called defenders of the true faith were doing and what is happening today in America.

We need to face the fact that America's claim to be a Christian nation is a misuse of the name of God. In times of war, domestic trouble, or natural disaster, we call upon God to defend, protect, and help us, but in our personal and private lives we want God to leave us to our selfishness and lust. We call ourselves a Christian nation, but in fact a majority of us are secular humanists and self-idolaters. We cannot continue misusing the name of God and avoid His correction.

I also believe that certain branches of the church in America are facing more serious consequences for their misuse of the name of God.

With the advent of liberal theology, many of America's clergy have adopted "brands" of Christianity that are alloyed and adulterated with belief systems that are not Christian at all. For instance, thanks to the Jungian thinking that has infiltrated many of our divinity schools and seminaries, theology students and pastoral candidates are often taught that we are all a mixture of light and dark. In this theology, that which is darkness in us is not necessarily bad or evil—it is just a motivation or drive that needs to be brought out so it can be integrated into our lives.

Recently the Episcopal Church has shown a particular disinterest in honoring the holy name of God by approving the appointment of its first openly gay bishop—even though God, in many places throughout the Bible, expressly forbids the practice of homosexuality. By going against God's commands, the Episcopal Church has said, in essence, "We take upon ourselves the name and authority of the church of Jesus Christ, and we are blessing what God has called unholy. We are taking it upon ourselves to stand in the place of God and place our approval upon an evil thing." By claiming to speak for God while defying God's Word, these men and women are spreading the mantle of the church over a practice that is ungodly. In the name of God, they are telling their congregations that it is all right to go against God's express commands.

Tragically, in doing so these Christian leaders are bringing condemnation not only upon themselves, but upon many of their followers as well. Rather than leading men and women away from this forbidden lifestyle, they are encouraging them to embrace it. Jesus warned false leaders like these when he said, "If anyone causes one of these little ones who believe in me to sin, it would be better for him to have a large millstone hung around his neck and to be drowned in the depths of the sea" (Matthew 18:6).

Even more dishonoring to the name of God are the now widespread reports of clergy who abuse members of their congregations. We are being bombarded with reports of ministers and priests who manipulate and coerce innocent people under their spiritual care to have sexual intercourse with them. The sad, angry faces of men, women, and children who were pressured to perform intimate and degrading acts with a spiritual leader who they trusted appear on our television screens almost weekly. What was done to them is beyond tragic. Someone who offered the appearance of the ultimate kind of safety—the refuge of what is meant to be a pure and holy relationship—turned out to be the very person with whom they were least safe. That kind of abuse of God's name must rank among the greatest of abominations, for the soul damage that is done to these victims is deep and sometimes lifelong. To those who have stood in the place of God and then put others through a living hell, the words "You shall not misuse the name of the LORD" are an offense. But because they have betrayed the sacred trust that comes with representing the name of God, they will pay a heavy price for their sins.

THE BLESSINGS OF HONORING GOD'S NAME

To honor someone is to think long and deep about his or her wonderful qualities. We speak reverently about that person to others. We create memorials to him or her.

In America, we are regaled by television programs that honor our celebrities, be they professional athletes, movie stars, singers, or musicians. More thoughtful programmers bring us stories about the lives of American heroes—men and women who came to greatness on the battlefield, or perhaps in politics, art, or social reform. The hosts of these shows take us into the lives of these people and cause us to consider what character traits make them notable. In a sense, they help us to pause and meditate on what makes for greatness.

When we honor the name of God—the great "I AM"—we engage in much the same kind of process, but we do it for the benefit of our soul. To honor God is to think long and deep about all the meanings in that wonderful and "unfinished" name "I AM." To reflect on His amazing qualities is to take them deeply into ourselves by meditating on them and pondering them the way you would study the facets of a gem by turning it in your hands and looking into its startling beauty.

When we honor God, we spend time considering the qualities about Him that make Him everything we need. Search the Bible and we will find various renderings of His name, each one adding a facet to his character. He is El Shaddai—God Almighty (Genesis 17:1). He is mighty enough to save us from any kind of trouble, no matter how impossible our situation may seem, and at the same time His position of supreme authority makes Him the God higher than all other gods that our souls long to serve. He is Jehovah-Jireh (Genesis 22:8), able to provide for our every need and also the One to whom we return thanks, seeding our souls with generosity and charity. He is Jehovah-Tsidkenu (Psalm 4:1), our righteousness and the One to whom we lead others who have lost their moral bearings and are in need of soul cleansing and salvation. "The name of the LORD is a strong tower. The righteous run to it and are safe" (Proverbs 18:10).

To honor God means more than contemplating Him, however. It also means, in the words of the Psalmist, to "magnify" His name (Psalm 34:3 KJV). To "magnify" God and His name is to make that which is invisible—His unseen qualities—see-able. It is to live in a way that allows others to catch glimpses of God because they see His character traits in us.

Judeo-Christian spirituality does not allow us to venerate God by mere ritual acts done in private, after which we can go back to "the real world" to live any way we choose. When we honor God, we do so not just with private meditations about the meanings of His name. We honor Him by the way we live our lives. In this way, we are blessed by honoring the name of God, because, as Paul said, then we share in His glory (2 Corinthians 3:18).

Can there be any greater blessing than to experience the presence of the God who lives in unapproachable light and to have the radiance of His glory shine through us? Or to be mirrors of His greatness to others in this dark, troubled world of people who are lost and wandering and in need?

There is another blessing that comes in honoring the name of God. Jehovah—the great I AM, higher than all other gods, above His own creation—is the ultimate ground of being. He cannot be moved or changed. There is nothing greater than God in which to place our trust. Not only that, He remains forever the same (Hebrews 13:8), and, as the Psalmist reminds us over and over, His love for us endures forever (Psalm 136:1). If we honor and fully grasp this aspect of God, we come to know at a deep level of our being that no matter what devastation, chaos, or loss is going on around us, He provides a solid place in spirit on which to stand. We have a God in whom we trust, the way little children implicitly trust their parents.

Once again, this blessing is not for us alone. When we are blessed with the understanding that God is unchanging and unshakable, we begin to emulate His characteristic integrity. We not only trust; we can be trusted. Others are blessed by God's stability and reliability that is being formed in us. Thus, we can take part in healing the wounds dealt to society.

Those who have trusted in anything that is lower than, or less than, the name of the true God will certainly be shaken. Stock markets fall and investments fail. Promised breakthroughs in medicine fail to come in time to save someone we love. Politicians take oaths of office and are caught in lies and deceit. Government officials betray public trust. Clergy lure innocents with promises of safety and violate their sacred offices. American society is wounded in spirit, and out of its wounds pour cynicism, bitterness, distrust, and a sense that we are all on our own with no one really to care for our good. But when those of us who trust in the name of God show integrity to a world that has seen precious little of it, we bring a spiritual balm to those who long to live in a nation where there is still virtue and true character.

And, yes, it is also wise to accept that His laws are unchanging, forever the same. Jesus said, "I am . . . the truth" (John 14:6). The rules by which God governs the universe and mankind do not shift from one era to the next. According to God's standard, wrong will always be wrong, and right will be right now and forever. If we do what is right, we will always be pleasing to Him.

Again, when we believe God's very name means righteousness, we will strive to live in right relationships with other people. By the way we act and treat other people, we show the world how to make "crooked paths"—all those twisted ways we deal with each other— become "straight." And so we bring to our relationships the blessing of freedom and openness in place of tension, and honesty in place of confusion and doubt.

When we honor and do not misuse the name of God, we experience profound blessings. Moreover, we are transformed in spirit and we become a blessing to others. We become, in Jesus' words, "the light of the world" (Matthew 5:14). We do so when, by honoring God's name with our lives, we help to heal the eyes of those who are spiritually blind because they see, however dimly, the reflection of God's glory in us.

Is this not what America needs?

SEVEN

Commandment Four: Observe a Sabbath Rest

Remember to observe the Sabbath day by keeping it holy.

—EXODUS 20:8 NLT

WHEN THE CHILDREN OF ISRAEL became slaves in Egypt, they were put under cruel taskmasters and forced to work seven days a week with no break. If they faltered, the Egyptian overseer was always present with the lash. If their quota of bricks was short, there was the lash. If they stumbled while pulling gigantic stones to build Pharaoh's pyramid, there was the lash. Day after endless day, their exhausted bodies cried out for relief. But there was no relief. There was no time to hope . . . no time to think . . . only endless, backbreaking labor.

Then God delivered the Ten Commandments to Moses on Mount Sinai, reminding the Israelites that they had been slaves in Egypt. Now one of the blessings of freedom was a day each week for rest, reflection, creative thought, and worship—a chance to meditate on the fact that their Creator brought forth the glory of creation in six days, and then on the seventh day He rested.

In case they misunderstood His message, God made it clear that keeping the Sabbath meant no plowing, no gathering, no gardening, no construction, no light or heavy labor, no commerce inside cities and towns, and no work outside. Their slaves were to rest, their animals were to rest, and their tools were to rest.

If this command seems burdensome, think what the life of a slave was like. Then consider what life would be like in America without a weekend. I shudder at the expression, "24-7." Human beings can't work seven days week-in and week-out without serious mental and physical exhaustion. We call it burnout. We must have a day off. We must have rest. We violate God's Fourth Commandment at our peril.

A Correct View of the Sabbath

By the time of Jesus Christ, narrow-minded religious leaders had developed an incredibly onerous body of rules about what a person could and could not do on the Sabbath. These religious leaders once rebuked Jesus and His disciples for walking through a field of grain on the Sabbath and munching on some of the seeds. Apparently, their Sabbath "rulebook" considered stripping the grain from the stalk to be work and therefore forbidden on the Sabbath. Jesus made clear that God did not establish the Sabbath for the purpose of creating an impossible straitjacket in which to confine people. Instead, Jesus declared, "The Sabbath was made for man, not man for the Sabbath" (Mark 2:27).

God intended the Sabbath rest to be a blessing, not a burden. Therefore, we should carefully avoid being legalistic about the Sabbath, lest we become like the oppressive religious leaders of Jesus's day. But we must also take equal care not to overemphasize the Sabbath rest and ignore the part of the commandment that says, "Six days you shall labor and do all your work . . ." (Exodus 20:9).

My father practiced a correct understanding of the Sabbath rest. He was a prominent public figure who became a senior United States senator. His capacity for hard work was legendary. He represented a state that today has over six million inhabitants, and he received thousands of letters from his constituents. Despite the volume of mail, he had an ironclad rule: No letter was to remain in his office unanswered longer than twenty-four hours. To my knowledge, no Virginia senator before or since ever set such a demanding standard for constituent service.

But my father, who was the son of a Baptist minister, had learned a great lesson that he shared with me. When I was putting CBN's first television station on the air, I was shorthanded and my personal workload was staggering. On top of that, I had a growing family with three, then four, young children. My father came to me and put some money in my hand. "This is for you personally," he said, "not for your ministry. I want you to use this money so that you and your wife from time to time can get away from your work and children to rest. You can never accomplish what you need to do unless you are rested and refreshed."

My father was a wise man, but his thoughts were shaped by his training in the Word of God. He practiced the Ten Commandments, and he experienced their blessings in his distinguished career.

THE BLESSING OF A SABBATH REST

The great promise of the Fourth Commandment is spelled out in detail by the prophet Isaiah, who wrote: "Keep the Sabbath day holy. Don't pursue your own interests on that day, but enjoy the Sabbath and speak of it with delight as the LORD's holy day. Honor the LORD in everything you do, and don't follow your own desires or talk idly. If you do this, the LORD will be your delight. *I will give you great honor and give you your full share of the inheritance I promised to Jacob, your ancestor. I, the LORD, have spoken!*" (Isaiah 58:13–14 NLT; emphasis added).

The promise to those who keep this commandment is great honor and a share of the inheritance promised to Jacob. Greater than that, those who obey this commandment find that the Lord is their delight. I have adopted Isaiah 58 as my own standard. I take a Sabbath rest every week. It is on this day while I rest and worship God that His Spirit begins to enlighten, encourage, and inspire me. When I worship God on the Sabbath, my mind can soar to a realm where difficult things become easy and the impossible becomes possible.

I am not speaking of exhausting religious exercises, meetings, church suppers, and planning sessions. I am talking about setting aside time for plain, old-fashioned, uninterrupted rest, prayer, meditation, and quiet Bible reading. The "heritage of Jacob" is a great blessing, and that is what is promised to those who keep the Sabbath. I personally want it, and so should you!

TAKING A DAY FOR SABBATH REST

The original Sabbath of the Hebrews of the Bible was Saturday. The Orthodox Jews still celebrate a Sabbath that begins at sundown on Friday and continues twenty-four hours until sundown on Saturday.

Sunday in biblical times was called "the first day of the week" (Acts 20:7; 1 Corinthians 16:2). Since this was the day of the resurrection of Jesus Christ, the early Christians—most of whom were Jewish—held their meetings on Sunday rather than Saturday. As custom developed, the Christian Sabbath, or day of rest and worship, became Sunday, and this was the day established by law in America. There was a time not long ago when Sunday was a very special day.

Mark, who is forty-three, remembers that as a boy growing up in a religious home in Ohio, his father intervened when he and his brother once wanted to build a birdhouse on Sunday. "Today is the Lord's day," his father said. "Why don't you go outside and play? And while you are outside, look around at the creation and remember that the Lord made all this for us to enjoy."

"I'm sure it's largely because my parents continually did things like that—focusing me on God and His creation, sending me out-side on Sunday afternoons where I'd think about God's amazing work in nature—that I found my career in environmental work. I believe God 'called' me to this work way back then, when I was a kid, outside alone, contemplating God in the woods and fields around our house."

Janet, a woman from California in her late thirties, holds the line with her family when it comes to what they do on Sunday. "When I was a kid—my goodness, it wasn't that long ago—my parents were shocked when the Sunday 'blue laws' began to change and stores started opening on Sunday. Now look at our culture. It's nonstop.

"But as for our family, we still don't shop on Sunday unless we're out of something that we absolutely need. My husband and I even monitor what the kids see on TV or at the movies, especially on Sunday. And we're in church. We don't miss worship unless someone's sick or some urgent matter comes up.

"I don't know how people do it," Janet concludes, "when they don't take a day to focus on the Lord and to get some rest."

Unfortunately, Mark and Janet are part of a vanishing minority in America.

COMMERCE ON THE LORD'S DAY

In America, keeping the Sabbath as "the Lord's day" has largely become an antiquated idea. But when the nation was founded, Americans took seriously God's commandment to keep the Sabbath holy.

In their book, *Blue Laws: The History, Economics, and Politics of Sunday-Closing Laws,* authors David Laband and Deborah Hein-buch give an historical account from the year 1789, telling of a certain man—in fact, a dignitary of great importance—who was forced because of urgent business to travel on the Sabbath. He started in Connecticut and needed to get to New York City. He and his entourage got up at daybreak, saddled their horses, and set off down the dirt roads leading south. They had not gotten very far before they were stopped by a local constable. Why, he demanded to know, were they taking a long journey—which he could see by the fact their horses were laden with traveling gear—on the Sabbath day? Everyone in the party knew, of course, about the laws that had been in effect since colonial days prohibiting "unnecessary travel, either by walking or riding" on the Sabbath.

The account goes on to say that the travelers narrowly missed a stay in a cold jail cell by explaining—truthfully, we hope—that while they were intending to carry on to New York the following day, they were going to break up their trip by stopping at the next town, where they planned to attend church services. Apparently, the constable bought the story because he allowed the men to continue on their journey.

What makes this account most extraordinary is that this party was headed by none other than the newly elected president of the United States, George Washington. What also makes it extraordinary is the fact that it demonstrates how solidly our nation was built upon the laws of God.

Hold this image of early American life in contrast with the attack on Sabbath-keeping that gained force, particularly in the 1960s. In 1961, the first of several legal battles reached the Supreme Court, challenging the honoring of Sunday as "the Lord's day" and "a day of rest" when businesses were to remain closed. At the time, the Supreme Court ruled in favor of keeping the so-called blue laws intact. But it did so by using a secular line of reasoning, stating that it was within the power of state legislatures to proclaim a weekly day of rest for laborers, and also that it was appropriate for that day of rest to be one that was preferred by the majority of a given state's citizens. The Court rejected arguments that blue laws violated the consciences of citizens who were compelled by their religion to worship on a Sabbath different than the one established by their state.

While it may appear that the U.S. Supreme Court justices were rendering an opinion that favored Judeo-Christian standards, in fact they were astutely sidestepping the issue. Their decision redirected all subsequent cases to the various state supreme courts, and there, of course, the erosion began. Numerous business interests began to lobby their state courts and legislatures to strike down their state's blue laws. As a result, from state to state, blue laws were repealed. In some cases, states made the claim they were not doing away with blue laws altogether, but just modifying them. What this amounted to in most cases was prohibiting the sale of alcohol on Sunday, though in some states merchants could begin selling wine after noon. This gave the appearance that legislators and judges were honoring the majority opinion held by Christians and honoring the Sabbath. In effect, however, this was merely a weak attempt to placate religious people, while giving the secular business interests what they demanded—the right to sell and work on Sunday.

So throughout the late 1960s and early 1970s, grocery stores and drug stores began to open on Sundays, followed by department and gift stores. America's day of rest slowly began to change. Consider where we are today.

One weekend not long ago, I drove past a shopping mall on a Sunday. To my surprise, it was probably busier than on any other day of the week. From the crowd in the parking lot and the loads of packages and bags people were hauling, it was plain this was not a day when a few folks had run out to pick up a few necessary items. This was clearly a major shopping day.

New York City has long been known as "the city that never sleeps." Now it seems the entire country never sleeps. As the courts have stripped us of our Christian heritage, the Sabbath day America once knew and honored has virtually disappeared. Commerce and entertainment are nonstop. Today, besides doing all the shopping you want, in most towns and cities you can get repair service, delivery service, cleaning service, and virtually any service you need on Sunday. An endless variety of on-line services has also emerged, reaching into our homes via the Internet and tempting us even farther away from sacred solitude.

A DAY THAT BELONGS TO GOD

Is Sunday still a special day in our culture? Yes, it is. But not in the way it was originally intended. In our thinking, Monday through Friday belongs to someone else—our school or our employer. Saturday belongs to household errands and to kids' sports. After that, most Americans seem to have the attitude that Sunday is the one day out of seven we get to do exactly what we want without anyone else placing demands on our time. Most of us—those who don't have to work weekends, at any rate—would likely say, "Sunday is my day." To that, God would say, "Yes, and no."

According to the God of the Bible, Sunday belongs to Him. First and foremost, when God set aside one day of the week for the Sabbath, He intended for us to take time out from all our other mental and physical activities to focus our body, mind, and soul on Him. Believers have honored this commandment in various ways throughout history—by attending liturgies, by hearing the Bible read and taught in church services, and by contemplating God and His Word on their own. However Christians have worshiped on this day throughout time, the point is that for centuries Sunday has been the one day that belongs *to the Lord.*

THE BLESSINGS OF THE LORD'S DAY

What blessings would we gain by honoring the Sabbath?

First, there is a practical benefit. Medical experts now know that stress is one of the factors contributing to the development of every major illness—from depression to allergies, to heart disease, to migraines, to immunological diseases like lupus and rheumatoid arthritis, to cancer. At the same time, studies have shown that those who set aside time regularly to be with the Lord and to seek spiritual community are mentally, emotionally, and physically healthier than people who do not take time for spiritual fellowship or private worship.

Second, and most importantly, there are spiritual benefits that come from Sabbath-keeping. Taking a day to refocus our souls upward, to the Lord, shifts our attention from the cares and demands of this temporal life to the peace and stability of the eternal world. Left to ourselves, we tend to focus on little things as if they are of major importance. Sabbath rest gives us a perspective on life that can only come when we lift our spirits out of the forest of everyday concerns.

By refocusing our attention on the Lord, we are also lifted above our self-centeredness. What a relief it is to escape the constant demands of self and be free to let our souls expand to take in the Lord's concerns for humanity, for other people, and for just and righteous causes. We are no longer consumed by mere self-concern and, instead, contribute to works that give our life meaning and purpose.

The One who made us knows that in the deep soul of man there is a void that only He can fill. Man's center is God. Because God is our Creator, He understands that with all the demands and pressures on us in these days, we become uncentered. We find ourselves saying things like: "I don't know what's the matter with me. Nothing is really wrong with my life, but nothing seems right, either." "I wish I could find my path in life. I wish I knew what I'm supposed to do." "My life is good in just about every way, so why does it seem so out of whack, like something's missing?"

Each of these statements, which we often hear in our culture, gives witness to the same fact: When we do not take time to make God the center of our lives, we lose our center. We become like phonograph records in which the hole has been cut in the wrong place so that it still spins, but the sound is distorted. Without a Sabbath rest, our lives become off-kilter and stressful.

A REMINDER OF GOD'S REST

This leads to another blessing we experience when we keep the Sabbath. God placed the Sabbath in our pathway every week as a real-time reminder of Himself. He cannot be seen by human eyes; nonetheless, He holds open a space in time for us to focus on Him. One day we shall see Him face to face and know Him as we are now known by Him—fully (1 Corinthians 13:12). For now, we are given one full day of the week to meet with Him in Spirit. In that regard, I love the wonderful statement of the apostle John, who wrote in the book of Revelation, "It was the Lord's Day, and I was worshiping in the Spirit. Suddenly, I heard a loud voice behind me. . . . I saw seven gold lampstands. And standing in the middle of the lampstands was the Son of Man" (Revelation 1:10, 12–13 NLT). To repeat, John was "in the Spirit" on the Lord's day, and he saw Jesus. If we do it right, this can be our reward.

Those who violate the Sabbath rest are only hurting themselves, yet they make excuses as to why they cheat themselves of a blessing. "Even though I work on Sunday, I take off another day of the week. Monday [or some other day] is my Sunday." But the truth is, it's very hard, if not impossible, to relax on another day of the week, because the machinery of society continues to grind. The culture aids and abets us, not only in ignoring time with God, but also in what amounts to self-abuse. It does so by continuing full-throttle, seven days a week, and offering us whatever we want while denying us what we actually need: rest.

But, as Jesus pointed out, the Sabbath is one of the greatest ways the God who created a covenant of love with His people offers us blessing.

Why, then, is the law of the Sabbath such an offense to our culture?

The Sabbath versus Sports and Shopping

Several years ago, my wife and I drove to a local restaurant at about six o'clock one Sunday evening in late January. The highway, which usually was filled with traffic at this time, was practically deserted. There were few signs of life anywhere. The restaurant, which customarily was crowded on a Sunday evening, was almost empty. It was eerily like the aftermath from an attack in wartime.

Then it dawned on me that the citizens of Virginia were joining 120 million of their fellow Americans who stayed home to worship by television at the national shrine called the Super Bowl. The best team in the National Football Conference was getting ready to play the best team in the American Football Conference. The number of people who gather each year to watch this game exceeds in magnitude any crowd assembled for any other activity in our nation.

And this unique Sunday is no longer the exception, but the rule. Each Sunday, muscular athletes fight for mastery in stadiums filled with tens of thousands of spectators screaming for one team or the other to propel an air-filled, laced pigskin down a field measuring one hundred yards. Citizens are taxed hundreds of millions of dollars to build the stadiums where this sport takes place. In fact, the reputation of the city involved seems to revolve around the success of its team and how many people come out to watch it play.

In America, the Sabbath no longer belongs to Jehovah God, but to the gods of professional sports. Every major tennis tournament schedules its finals on Sunday. The Professional Golfers Association begins play on Thursday, then plays Friday, then Saturday, with a hotly fought final round on Sunday.

Any family that tries to schedule a big family dinner on Sunday will soon find that the men in the family slip away one by one to the television room to check on the Redskins or the Cowboys or the Broncos. Or perhaps they want to see if Tiger Woods can prevail with some magical golf shot over the likes of V. J. Singh or Jim Furyk or Ernie Els.

People arrange to attend an early church service on Sunday so they can get home in time to make a golf tee time or a Little League game or the opening kickoff of a televised football game. A huge number of people have a massive Sunday edition of their local newspaper delivered to their homes. They sleep late, eat a leisurely brunch, and spend hours reading the paper.

Billions of dollars are invested in professional sports. The value of such teams as the Washington Redskins is in the $950 million range. The cost of a major league stadium can be $250 to $300 million. Private boxes in the stadium can lease for $100,000 or more each year. Star athletes can receive long-term compensation in excess of $100 million. The television rights to broadcast Sunday games run to several billion dollars a year. A thirty-second commercial during the Super Bowl will sell in 2004 for $2.4 million. That works out to $80,000 *per second!*

In addition to salaries or prize money, professional athletes are paid staggering sums to appear in product promotions. Tiger Woods was paid $1 million just to show up for a German golf tournament. His prize winnings are close to $6.5 million, yet his total annual income may come out closer to $60 million when fees for promotional endorsements are included.

Can anyone even consider the outrage that would be expressed in America if somebody dared suggest that Sunday should be a day of rest for the nation and that professional sports should be shifted to another day? Talk about an offense! Such a suggestion is unthinkable in postmodern America.

But the value of professional sports pales alongside the total value of shopping malls, strip malls, retail shops, department stores, restaurants, and hotels. We are not talking here in terms of hundreds of billions, but trillions, of dollars of value. The owners of these establishments calculate how much gross revenue they receive on a daily basis. Six times that sum is one amount. Seven times that amount is about 15 percent more. Fifteen percent more business means that their fixed investment is spread over a bigger base. Their profit per sale goes up. So, of course, they want their business running seven days a week. It's too bad if their employees can't attend church. It's too bad that their workers are exhausted without a real day of rest. It's too bad if shoppers never have a commerce-free day when society is at rest. What counts to them is the bottom-line profit.

Of course, these secularly minded businessmen don't consider that if they treat the Sabbath as a delight rather than an offense, the God who created the universe can give them more business in six days than they would receive in seven in defiance of His commandment.

AN EXAMPLE OF GOD'S BLESSING

A wonderful example of God's blessing on those who observe the Sabbath is the success of my friend Truett Cathy, the founder and principal owner of a fast-food restaurant chain called Chick-fil-A. Truett Cathy believed that he could provide a delicious sandwich by placing a generous filet of white-meat chicken on a roll and serving it to his customers along with the necessary accompaniments.

Truett was a dedicated Christian who believed that it was a violation of the Fourth Commandment to do business on Sunday or to make his employees work on Sunday. He believed that if he operated just six days a week, God would prosper him more than if he did business for seven days.

But Truett didn't take into account the commercial practices of the large malls where he tried to locate his Chick-fil-A restaurants. You see, big shopping malls create a massive commercial environment, so they don't merely want to lease retail spaces for a fixed rent. They want a fixed rent plus a percentage of the gross receipts of each of their tenants. To them, a six-day-a-week business would gross less than a seven-day-a-week business and therefore pay a lower rental.

So Truett had to guarantee that six days for his restaurant would be as profitable as seven days for a comparable business. To say that he did a lot of praying for God's blessing would be an understatement. But the miracle happened. The Chick-fil-A restaurants were so popular that in six days each week their gross revenues far exceeded the seven-day comparables.

To this day, Chick-fil-A, which now has over a thousand locations, is a booming business. Its gross revenues and net profits far exceed what Truett Cathy could have expected when he sold his first filet of white-meat chicken on a bun decades ago. And, of course, none of Truett Cathy's chain of fast-food restaurants is open on the Sabbath. To Truett Cathy and his employees, the Sabbath is a delight. He knows the heritage of Jacob.

GOD KNOWS BEST

In sum, the God who made us knows what will benefit us and what will harm us. Yet in our mad pursuit of money and success, Americans have come to believe that God does not know what He is talking about. We think that His laws stand in the way of our achieving what we believe is the materialistic "American dream." The Fourth Commandment is an offense to commerce, entertainment, and sports.

The legacy we have received in return is a nation hooked on painkillers, alcohol, and narcotics. We are a nation that is overworked and stressed out. Our homes are in shambles, our teenagers are neglected and in rebellion, and our psychologists can't seem to keep up with the demand of emotionally frazzled people. We join the chorus of those crying out, "Stop the world; I want to get off!"

In short, while keeping the Sabbath is an offense to our fast-paced culture, failing to take a day of rest as commanded by God causes us to miss tremendous benefits that could be ours. By not honoring the Sabbath, we are missing out on blessings that would keep strong the fabric of our nation, our communities, our families, and ourselves.

As the Psalmist wrote, in a time of worship and rest in the Lord:

> Keep me safe, O God, for in you I take refuge. . . . I have set the LORD always before me. Because He is at my right hand I will not be shaken. Therefore, my heart is glad and my body also will rest secure. . . . You have made known to me the path of life; you fill me with joy in your presence, with eternal pleasures at your right hand. (Psalm 16:1, 8–11)

We therefore should ask ourselves, Will we receive the blessing of the Lord and the heritage of Jacob, or will we experience emotional burnout? The choice is ours.

EIGHT

Commandment Five:
Honor Your Parents

Honor your father and your mother, as the LORD your God has commanded you, so that you may live long and that it may go well with you in the land which the LORD your God is giving you.

—DEUTERONOMY 5:16

THE FIRST FOUR COMMANDMENTS set the stage for all human relationships. The First Commandment establishes that there is no other universal Creator besides Jehovah. For the good of His people, God will not permit worship of other gods to divert His people from the truth.

The Second Commandment forbids the creation of any manmade object of worship because any such thing diminishes our understanding of God and the holiness and purity of life that worship of Him requires.

The Third Commandment forbids us to cheapen His presence in our lives by the flippant use of His name or by using His name to make Him a party to falsehood and curses. His people must receive answers to prayer in His name. Prayer is impossible to those who fail to reverence the source of His blessing.

Finally, the Fourth Commandment directs God's people to focus on the majesty not only of His person, His character, and His name, but His work of creation. To that end, He specifies that we are to have a day of refreshing and rest each week so we can be free to contemplate the majesty of the One who made "all that is" in six days, then ceased labor on the seventh.

From these commandments, we not only learn to focus on our Creator, but we are changed into His very nature. God says, "Be holy, for I am holy" (1 Peter 1:16). As we learn to love Him, we absorb His sublime ethical standards, which then become the basis of all laws and actions for the benefit of our fellow man.

The first four commandments are about our relationship to God. The last five are about the duties we owe to one another. The Fifth Commandment—which we will now explore—provides the basis for civil government, which begins with the family, then the clan, then the tribe, and then the nation.

THE AUTHORITY OF THE FAMILY

In every society, the family is the essential unit. If the integrity of families is destroyed, then the cohesion that binds towns, cities, and nations begins to disintegrate. Former education secretary William Bennett said it clearly: ". . . The traditional American family is the first, best and original Department of Health, Education and Welfare."

According to Jehovah God, the next in line of authority from Him are parents. We are to honor (or give weight to) our father and mother. Martin Luther wrote that this commandment refers to "those who are the representatives to God. Therefore, as God is to be served with honour and fear, His representatives are to be so too."

Parents are not only the authors and preservers of their children, but the Bible tells us that the father is to be the high priest of his family, capable of drawing wisdom and authority from God and transmitting them to his children.

The Bible tells us that all families on earth are to take their name from the Fatherhood of God. That is why Jesus Christ always referred to Jehovah as "Father." When His disciples asked Jesus to instruct them in prayer, He taught them to say, "Our Father in heaven, hallowed be your name" (Matthew 6:9).

All government stems from the relation of father and child, and, according to one nineteenth-century commentator, "draws its moral weight and stability, upon which the prosperity and well being of the nation depends from the reverence of children toward their parents." Without question, a child forms his conception of the nature of God from what he sees in his parents. Is the father kindly or overbearing, understanding or intemperate, considerate or indifferent? Does he uphold a standard of right living and discipline or cut moral corners and let his child grow up rebellious and undisciplined?

Many are the fathers and mothers who do a good job introducing their children to God in His many dimensions. They do so, not just by teaching their children to pray or to worship or to hear God's voice in the Scriptures, but also by their loving example and steadfast moral character. Their tenderness and their firmness form a kind of solid ground for a child's soul to stand upon. They embrace their children with a love that is constant and unwavering. At the same time, they train their children to obey moral laws and to live ethically. Fortunate is the child whose parents strive to offer him or her both love and discipline, because that child has been given not a perfect, but a much clearer, window to the character of God.

PARENTS WHO FALL SHORT OF GOD'S IDEAL

There are many parents, of course, who fall short of the ideals of godly parenting. They think they're being loving, when really they are consistently too weak to stand up to their children's need for boundaries and training. The children of these parents will picture a God who is mostly kind and sympathetic and who lets discipline slide. On the other hand, some parents are too strict or too harsh in their discipline. The children of these parents will imagine God is uncaring, impatient, and maybe even cruel sometimes. These children are at something of a disadvantage in life, because they will lack either self-control or empathy.

There are also parents who, sadly, do the poorest job imaginable. These are the parents who are caught up in self-indulgence and either neglect or abuse their children. They may be pushovers in their so-called love, giving into a child's worst attributes like temper or raw appetites. Or they may take advantage of their children, using them emotionally or even physically for their own selfish gratification.

Heather was the only daughter of parents who gratified their own worst attributes at her expense. From the time she was thirteen, her father abused her sexually. And when, at fifteen, Heather became pregnant, her mother drove her to an abortion clinic and left her there alone to go through the ordeal of abortion. "Here's the money you'll need," she said, handing her a fistful of bills. "They'll take care of you inside. I'll be back in a couple of hours to get you. And remember," her mother said, "this happened because you were messing around with a boyfriend."

Sadly, Heather's heartbreaking story, which she poured out to her pastor after he'd preached a sermon on the Fifth Commandment, can be repeated thousands of times. "And *now*," she said through angry tears, "God's telling me I have to 'honor my father and mother'?" Yes, her pastor replied. She would honor her parents by getting healing for her soul and by honoring the life they created . . . hers. But she would hear none of that. "My life is horrible, and it's their fault. And if it takes me the rest of my life, I'm going to make them see that they're *nothing*. Because that's how they made me feel."

This woman's resistance to God's commandment is echoed millions of times over in America. In various ways, by acts of aggression or negligence, children of all ages dishonor their parents and treat them as if they're of no importance, and sometimes as if they are nothing. Heather's story points out one of the main reasons that God's Fifth Commandment causes offense.

WHEN PARENTS ARE UNKNOWN OR ABUSIVE

How does the Fifth Commandment apply to children who are born from artificial insemination? How do we tell a child to honor the sperm of an unknown donor inseminated from a test tube? Who do we tell a kid born in a ghetto to honor when his mother has been promiscuous with so many men that she is unable to identify the father of her child? Or how do we teach a child of divorce to honor his or her mother and father when each of them stops at nothing to turn the loyalty of the child away from the ex-spouse?

How do we teach a child to honor a father who in drunken rages regularly beats his mother? How do we teach a child to honor an alcoholic or drug-addicted parent who throws him out to fend for himself at age thirteen? How do we teach a child to honor a parent who is a child-molesting sexual predator?

In short, American society is reaching a point where we have torn the Fifth Commandment to shreds. Without its restraining influence, the long-term life of our nation is placed in serious peril. But do the public schools and the courts reinforce or undermine the commandments? Here are a few examples that are indicative of trends.

UNDERMINING PARENTS

At seventeen, Kara became an emancipated minor. A California court ruled in her favor when, aided by a civil liberties group, she filed a lawsuit against her parents for being "oppressive." Her reasons? After the fourth time she was caught using drugs, and after the sixth time she was picked up for shoplifting, they had "forced" her to be schooled at home. They also "violated her rights" by forbidding her to see a number of the kids from her old crowd because

the kids were on probation for various crimes, from assault to larceny to dealing drugs.

What is tragic is that neither the civil liberties lawyers who won
Kara her emancipation, nor the judge who granted it, were there to
help Kara when, a year later, she delivered a baby and the twenty-
eight-year-old father refused to take responsibility for her or for the
child.

"Where are these men now," Kara's father asks, angrily, "when
we're left with the responsibility of helping our daughter pick up
the pieces of her life?"

In Virginia, ten-year-old Thomas tells his Christian parents at
the dinner table one evening that "praying is stupid." He says he
learned that from his school's guidance program, which is mandated by his state's legislature.

In class that day, the guidance teacher had asked Thomas's fifth-
grade class what they would do if they were playing with a ball in
the house when they'd been forbidden to, and they accidentally
broke a lamp. Some of his classmates said they'd hide the pieces and
some said they'd blame their little brother or the cat. Thomas and
one other Christian classmate said they would pray and ask God to
forgive them for disobeying their parents. The teacher then asked
the class to vote on which solution they thought was best. When no
one besides Thomas and his friend voted that prayer was the best
choice, a strong message was impressed on this little boy. "Everyone else thinks praying is stupid."

When Thomas's father met with the guidance teacher to tell her
the effects of her lesson, she brushed off his objections. "We're just
helping your child clarify his own values. That's what this guidance
program is mandated to do. Children need to own their own values."

When this father objected, saying that having children vote as to
whether they think prayer is a good or bad thing was tantamount to
running a popularity contest, the teacher continued to ignore his

concerns. "You and your wife may place a high value on faith and prayer, but maybe Thomas does not," she insisted. "We have to let our children find their own beliefs. We can't force our values or our morals upon them."

It is hardly surprising that both Kara's lawyers and Thomas's guidance teacher took the stance that the parents were "forcing" them to do something against their will. For decades now, a liberal viewpoint has been taking hold in the American legal and educational systems. To be sure, some states still stand by traditional family values, but throughout America the tide has eroded parental authority. "Honor your father and mother" is an offense to many people in these United States, where the individual is considered supreme and independent.

And yet among America's young people, juvenile delinquency, crime, and psychological disorders are higher than at any other time in our nation's history. Many blame the fact that parents are too overwhelmed by life's demands—by making ends meet or working out troubled marriages—or they're ill-equipped or just plain lazy. They argue that if parents are not going to do the job of parenting, then the state must step in and take over. If we look beyond this popularly held view, we'll see that other forces have been at work, moving against parental authority.

PARENTAL AUTHORITY

What has happened in America regarding the role of parents is nothing short of a quiet and largely unseen societal revolution. Though the family has long been the primary building block on which our society has grown strong, most recently, the authority of parents has been undermined. Of course, concerned conservative voices have been hard at work on behalf of the American family. That is because strong families, governed by loving and firm parents, work to everyone's best interest by creating healthy, productive, self-governing individuals. But more often, the negligent parent, not the diligent one, has been overused as a model by legislators, educators, lawyers, and liberal advocacy groups to "demonstrate" why children need to be more independent of their families. The prevailing sentiment among too many liberal (and influential) voices in America is that young people need to be freed from parental authority.

Unfortunately, even in certain elements within the church, the idea of honoring one's parents has lost the immediacy and power of a divine command. It is not seen as important to honor your father and mother. What's important is to psychoanalyze your relationship to your parents. Was your father too dominant and demanding, or too passive and weak? Was your mother too smothering or not caring enough? Were your parents there for you or absent? Helpful though it may be to gain insight into the dynamics of one's childhood, many Christians are never taught why God clearly instructed us, not primarily to *understand,* but to *honor* our father and mother.

THE BLESSING OF THE FIFTH COMMANDMENT

The Fifth Commandment, according to the apostle Paul, is the first commandment with promise: "That you may live long in the land the LORD your God is giving you" (Exodus 20:12; cf. Ephesians 6:2). Does that promise apply to the nation? I believe so, since the commandment was addressed to the entire nation. In the Fifth Commandment, God tells the people of Israel that the ongoing stability and longevity of their new nation in the Promised Land will depend on a cohesive society that reverences successor generations of their parents and patriarchs. God promises to bless with a long and stable life those who honor their parents, and He extends that same promise of blessing to any nation that will follow His command.

A nation that refuses to honor its parents does so at its own peril. Rebellious children who fail to honor their parents' instructions often begin to steal and murder, or engage in drunkenness or promiscuous sex. How many young lives are cut short by reckless driving, drunkenness, sexually transmitted diseases, gang warfare, crime, or poor dietary habits? It is honor to mothers and fathers that ensures a long life for a nation and for individuals.

Consider this example of a nation that chose to honor its patriarchs. When he was sixty-eight years old, my wife's father retired as a vice president of a company that manufactured paint. Because he was still quite vigorous, he went overseas with my mother-in-law to Beirut, Lebanon, where he established Sipes International Paint Company, the Middle East subsidiary of his U.S. company. He oversaw the construction of a factory in Beirut for Sipes International to sell paint and industrial finishes throughout the Middle East to such Persian Gulf states as Kuwait, Bahrain, Qatar, and Saudi Arabia.

My father-in-law was an active man who wasn't content to sit in an office but enjoyed getting out on the factory floor with the men to lift the buckets of pigments, oil, and solvents that made up each batch of paint. However, in the Middle East, he found that this was not possible. His Middle Eastern employees had such respect for a seventy-year-old man that as a mark of honor they refused to let him do any menial work. He was the patriarch, and they would lift, haul, and push for him, because in that culture a man of age is considered to be a repository of wisdom and therefore a venerated treasure.

This was certainly the biblical attitude toward the elderly grandfather, great-grandfather, or great-great grandfather. He was to be venerated, and his word was law. His blessing (or curse) would determine the destiny of his progeny after him.

Such honor is not unusual. It is built into the very fabric of the society of many civilizations. Shouldn't this honor also be our heritage in America?

THOSE WHO AVOID THEIR DUTY TO PARENTS

When Jesus Christ was on earth, he faulted the religious leaders of His day for devising religious customs that allowed them to break the commandment to honor mothers and fathers. To Jesus, the Fifth Commandment did not merely extend to obeying the instructions of parents. The commandment clearly extended to a positive duty to care for the well-being of parents when they have become old and unable to care for themselves.

Consequently, custom and regulation developed that a certain part of the income of grown children was to be used to support elderly parents. This requirement became a burden for ungrateful children, and the Pharisees were quick to provide a biblical-sounding way out. They told children wishing to duck their obligations to determine how much they should provide to support their parents. Then they could come to the temple and make a holy-sounding declaration that this sum was "corban," or dedicated to God. Therefore, it was no longer available to support their parents (see Mark 7:9–13). The trick in all this was the timing. Nothing was given to God in the present. It was a pledge of assets payable at death. While the children lived, the parents got nothing, the temple got nothing, and they could use their money as they pleased.

In condemning the trick, Jesus underscored the duty. Children have a duty to support their parents in their old age. As the apostle Paul put it, "If anyone does not provide for his relatives, and especially for his immediate family, he has denied the faith and is worse than an unbeliever" (1 Timothy 5:8).

I heard of a family of four grown children with an infirm mother. These children complained bitterly that, with their own family obligations, they couldn't possibly find the money to support their mother. A commentator who learned of this said, "Isn't it remarkable? One woman can feed, clothe, house, and educate four children, yet four children find it impossible to care for one woman."

CONSEQUENCES OF NEGLECTING OUR PARENTS

An entire volume can be written on this issue because it is looming like a cloud over the long-range financial stability of not only the United States, but Europe, Russia, and Japan. In all of these societies, the apostles of birth control and abortion have done a thorough job. The birthrate has fallen below replacement level in all but the United States. Many of the baby boom generation decided not to have children. An estimated forty-five million abortions over the past thirty years, along with the serious breakup of the nuclear family, has led to a demographic dilemma of major proportions that will begin hitting our society after the year 2010.

In the United States, the fastest-growing segment of our population, in terms of percentage growth, is made up of people over eighty. Europe, Russia, and Japan are experiencing critical demographic problems as their population growth has stalled and the percentage of their population considered elderly grows dramatically.

When Social Security was first introduced in the United States, there were approximately forty-five workers for every retiree. In the 1980s, that number dropped to four workers per retiree. When the huge number of baby boomers reaches retirement age, the ratio could be two to one. When that happens, the retirement tax on the active workforce could approach a staggering 23 percent of America's payrolls. Frankly, what staves off disaster in the United States is the large number of immigrant workers who come here from Asia and Latin America.

However, there is no such countervailing immigration in Western Europe, Russia, and Japan. In those nations, unless something is done quickly to rectify the situation, the burden of health and retirement expenses for their elderly population will be insupportable. They will be facing either national bankruptcy or grinding poverty or both. In all of these nations, it is clear that children have passed off their obligations to their parents, and the government has undertaken the duty of the children.

In America, politicians absolutely refuse to deal forcefully with this looming problem. The political clout of senior citizens, of which I am one at seventy-three years of age, is too great. They are well informed, highly motivated, and very politically active. Any political leader who attempts to fix the problem of Social Security in an intelligent way is punished in the next election by those elderly who cry out, "You can't take away my money!"

The trouble is that the politicians have already taken away their money. All of the money paid into Social Security has been spent to balance the federal budget. There is no Social Security Trust Fund. Social Security is now a transfer system from active workers to retirees. The Trust Fund is nothing but a gigantic IOU from the federal government to be paid off in future years by raising taxes on younger workers. I have seen many estimates of the potential liability, but according to the Concord Coalition, in 2002 it was $11.2 trillion for Social Security. Together with Medicare, the total unfunded liabilities in just these two "entitlement" programs were a staggering $24.1 trillion, a sum more than twice the entire U.S. economy and roughly four times the national debt. Frankly, when numbers get that large, they begin to lose their meaning; but suffice it to say, they present a serious threat to the long-term economic future of the nation and could help cascade a catastrophic collapse worse than the Great Depression.

At its inception, Social Security was a blessed stopgap to help desperately poor people who were trapped by the economic chaos of the Depression's aftermath. It is still a blessing to millions. However, when our country was founded, families took the Fifth Commandment seriously and cared for their own. Families looked after each other and neighbors helped neighbors. Somehow this nation did very well from 1607 until the 1930s without a gigantic federal government and a taxpayer-funded system of ever more generous entitlements. Then the Fifth Commandment became a national offense as government relieved children of their biblical responsibilities.

Perhaps it is too late to reestablish in our society the concept that caring for the elderly is the responsibility of children, not the federal government. For the vast majority of our society, we need a system of compulsory, tax-deductible retirement and health savings accounts. As a nation, we should spend whatever it takes to promote intact families, sexual abstinence outside of marriage, and the firm belief that children have a clear duty to care for their parents.

WAYS SOCIETY CAN CARE FOR ELDERLY PARENTS

Of course, our society can care for the disabled, the widow, the orphan, and the truly destitute. The homeless poor shouldn't have to sleep on sidewalks or the jobless try to survive by eating out of garbage cans. There can be a partnership between government and the thousands of private agencies in our society to give relief, job training, and hope to those less fortunate. For example, for this purpose, I took the commands of Isaiah 58:6–7 very seriously and founded Operation Blessing International Relief and Development. In the private sector, we have taught about 300,000 inner-city youth to read, have provided free medical care to some 850,000 people worldwide, are providing crucial employment skills to the unemployed, and at present are delivering over four million pounds of food for the poor and elderly in the inner cities and Appalachia each month.

The dramatic success of legislation in the 1990s to reform welfare by moving the poor from welfare to the job force shows that strong action can help solve what seemed like an intractable problem.

Many states found that men were fathering children and then leaving the mother and children to become wards of the state or the federal government. There was a simple solution to the problem: a "Fugitive Father Act." Fathers who abandon their clear responsibilities are to be apprehended and compelled either to support their children or to go to jail. These laws seem harsh, but they are just and they work.

If children refuse to support their elderly parents as the Lord commands them to do, what would prevent the state or federal government from putting in place regulations requiring children to support their destitute parents? The average man with all his strength cannot lift a good-sized refrigerator by himself. However, thirty men using just their index finger can lift the same load as if by magic. Our nation is facing a load that will soon become insupportable. If every child begins to take a small share of caring for elderly parents, that care plus private savings and the assistance of private-sector relief and modest government help, will make lifting our nation's load dramatically easier.

All it will take is obedience to a commandment meant for our good. If we truly honor our parents, we will experience all the blessings of the Fifth Commandment.

NINE

Commandment Six:
Respect Human Life

You shall not murder.

—Exodus 20:13

WHEN WE VIEW the Ten Commandments in their full context, it becomes clear that they were intended above all else to ensure a society with proper values, an enduring structure, and the ability of all the people to live free from fear.

The Sixth through the Tenth Commandments begin "You shall not," which clearly implies either that the people already had been doing these things and should stop, or that they had within themselves tendencies that needed to be restrained so that the conduct did not begin.

Years ago I shared the view of most people that the Ten Commandments were a series of negative commands meant to restrain. But as I studied them more deeply, I realized that obedience to them gives a wonderful sense of peace to a community when it realizes that there exists a power to prevent anyone from inflicting harm to life, property, marriage, or reputation.

OUR MOST PRECIOUS POSSESSION

Without question, the most precious possession that each of us enjoys is our life. Recently, vicious forest fires struck California, burning a land area larger than the state of Rhode Island and destroying at least two thousand homes and their contents. Although the people interviewed on television were saddened by the loss of their possessions, without exception their humbling response was, "We are still alive, and we can rebuild." Possessions can be destroyed, but not the human spirit. There is life, and there is hope!

When the framers of the Declaration of Independence enumerated the inalienable rights given us by our Creator, the first was life, then liberty, and then the pursuit of happiness. If a person is dead, no amount of political liberty or ability to pursue happiness does him any good. So when a wise Creator set forth five commandments to protect people, to ensure their peace of mind He first prohibited killing. "You shall not murder." Life is not only the highest earthly possession, but it is made in the image of God and is His unique creation, even when under attack.

Since the Law of Moses clearly mandates executions for crimes and specifies certain military actions, it is clear that this commandment forbids murder, not capital punishment or killing in battle. Murder, in its essence, is the premeditated taking of the life of another. In the case of accidental death or death from self-defense, the Law of Moses allowed the guilty party to flee to a city of refuge where the vengeful relative of the deceased could not reach him (Numbers 35:22–25). Since there is no direct object listed after the verb "murder," Bible commentators believe correctly that the commandment "You shall not murder" also applies to killing yourself by suicide.

These five commandments are no longer an age-old fantasy. Tourists at the Washington Hilton in one of the most fashionable parts of the nation's capital were warned not to leave the hotel on foot except in groups of four or five to avoid muggers who might kill, rape, or rob. I stayed in a hotel in New York City, where, if memory serves me correctly, there were either three or four supplemental deadbolts on the door in addition to the standard hotel door lock, deadbolt, and chain. People now live in fear behind locked and barred doors for fear of rape, robbery, and murder.

In 2003 the Allied Coalition won a startlingly quick victory in Iraq, but more than water, electricity, and schools, the people asked for law and order so that they and their families would be safe from lawless mobs who were roaming the streets looting and killing. No society can function if lawless mobs rule the streets.

But in twenty-first-century America, God's commandment protecting life has been blurred. Instead of a culture celebrating life, we have become a culture celebrating death—death of the unborn and the death of the elderly.

AMERICANS' "RIGHT TO CHOOSE"

The liberty of self-actualization, not life, has become the most important right an individual can have. In America, a woman's personal freedom, her "right to choose," has taken priority over the right of the child in her womb to live its life. Whereas the founders of our nation took God's Sixth Commandment seriously, recognizing that life is the single most important personal gift He gives, the liberal faction today insists that the right to personal freedom is preeminent.

As a result of our insistence upon liberty over life, America has developed a sort of schizophrenia in regard to the taking of life.

On one hand, we are outraged when misguided young men blow up a federal office building in Oklahoma, wiping out innocent lives, including those of children and infants in a daycare center. We are disgusted when two youths in Wyoming tie a third to a fence and beat him to death, and we are horrified when two snipers stalk our nation's capital and surrounding areas, killing people at random and in cold blood, apparently for sport. Most especially, we are numb with pain and grief when foreign terrorists crash jetliners into the World Trade Center, the Pentagon, and a field in western Pennsylvania, murdering thousands. Clearly, as a nation, we are still against the murder of some people.

On the other hand, there are types of murder to which we have become virtually numb. Since 1973, when the Supreme Court legalized abortion with the *Roe v. Wade* decision, the lives of as many as forty-five million American children have been terminated in doctors' offices, clinics, and hospitals. It is monstrous what we as a free, democratic, and mostly Christian country have allowed. But in the face of this, while one of the greatest mass murders in history is happening on our own soil, we are mostly silent. We allow it by taking away personhood and legal protection from the unborn, who liberals say are not babies but fetuses.

And so there are millions of Americans who insist it is wrong to limit a woman's right to choose abortion, and wrong to prevent someone from committing assisted suicide if he or she is terminally ill. They ignore God's command, "You shall not murder," and insist upon the sovereignty of the individual.

THE BLESSING OF THE SIXTH COMMANDMENT

On the surface, this commandment is a great protection for each one of us against the anger and vengeful impulses of other people. When law is weak, murderous anger and revenge killings turn societies into jungles.

In the 1990s I formed a company that received a license to do business in direct-to-home television across all of Russia. My partner was TASS Telecom, which was a subsidiary of the Russian government's publicity arm, TASS. I was told that every business in Russia needed a "roof." Without TASS as our "roof," we would be victimized by the Russian mafia.

While I was in Moscow, my associates took me to dinner at the Planet Hollywood restaurant. The owner was a naturalized U.S. citizen originally from Bangladesh. He told me how the law of the jungle worked for him in Moscow. He had noticed a shortage of highly prized American merchandise in Moscow, so he opened a huge emporium full of merchandise, called The USA Store.

On opening day he expected trouble, so he hired 1,000 ex-soldiers and ex-KGB officers and positioned them, armed with automatic weapons, in front of his store. Trouble came soon after the store opened, when a flotilla of black sedans arrived and disgorged scores of fully armed Russian mafia expecting to be paid protection money to furnish him a "roof." The armed groups faced each other, but no shots were fired. When the mobsters realized that they were outmanned and outgunned, they got back in their cars and drove away. Except for a little grease money to local officials, this was his last encounter with the criminals.

But who wants to live in a society where the weak pay protection money or die? Where there is no defense except from your own militia? This is the law of the frontier as depicted in Hollywood westerns where life is cheap. As hard as it is to believe, testimonies from Iraqi citizens indicate a preference for a strong, even ruthless, dictator rather than the lawless rule of the jungle where no one is safe.

Considering America's current disregard for the value of life in violation of the Sixth Commandment, how far away are we from becoming like these lawless nations?

LIFE COMES FROM THE LORD

In the Psalms, David was inspired by God's Spirit to affirm that the gift of life comes from the Lord. In Psalm 139, David writes, "For you created my inmost being" (v. 13). Later he declares that God is intimately involved in the creation of every child's physical being, but at this point he is telling us, by divine revelation, that God is the Creator of every living *soul.* This tells us that our very personhood, the essence of who we are, is a gift from the Father.

God knows even the circumstances of our birth, and they are

part of His divine plan for each life. He inspired David to write: "You brought me out of the womb" (Psalm 22:9). And also: "All the days ordained for me were written in your book before one of them came to be" (Psalm 139:16).

Hebrew wisdom, inspired by God, has given the world a great gift: the concept that every human life is valuable. Jesus emphasized the value God places even upon lives that make no appreciable contribution and that we would count as unworthy from our human perspective. He said, "Look at the birds of the air; they do not sow or reap or store away in barns, and yet your heavenly Father feeds them. Are you not much more valuable than they?" (Matthew 6:26).

Clearly, God not only holds the supreme right to make decisions about our lives, but He also has a love for life. We can trust that the decisions He makes regarding our personal circumstances are good, despite what they may seem in our eyes.

To the liberal mind, such talk is objectionable, and for many average Americans who are treated almost daily to liberal rhetoric in the media, such talk feels uncomfortable. The war cry of the American individual is, "But it's my body and my life, and I can do what I want with it!"

LITTLE VALUE FOR HUMAN LIFE

Why is the Sixth Commandment, "You shall not murder," such an offense today?

Even at the surface level of American popular culture, we can see that life is seen to have less and less value. View our films or listen to our popular music, and the violence is appalling. Estimates are that, by the time a youth in America reaches eighteen years of age, he or she will have witnessed an appalling 200,000 acts of violence on television alone. Even our children's video games, like the ultra-violent *Grand Theft Auto* and *Man Hunt,* celebrate bloodletting and the senseless, sickening destruction of human life. Proclaiming our right to choose our own way of life and our own means of entertainment, we are choosing to celebrate violence and death. Indulging ourselves in destructive fantasies and bizarre games has become our leisure-time activity.

In this climate, "You shall not murder" is a statement to be mocked. "Lighten up," say the liberal proponents of free speech and expression. "We have a right to be entertained any way we want." We are supposed to ignore the fact that the two boys who committed mass murder at Columbine High School in Littleton, Colorado, had apparently been desensitized to murder by violent computerized video games. We are to overlook that these games are similar to virtual-reality videos used by the military to help soldiers —who are preparing to enter combat—overcome their natural aversion to killing another human being.

The fact that we can view such violence as entertainment is a signal that deep beneath the cultural landscape a dangerous shift has taken place in our attitude toward life.

The Quality of Life As Supreme

In America, we no longer believe that the right to life itself is our first right. Instead we have shifted our stance and now insist that, along with the right to personal freedom, the right to determine our own *quality of life* is supreme. Anything I choose to do to improve the "quality" of my own life has become the governing attitude.

On the surface, having the freedom to act on our own behalf and choose our quality of life seems like a very good thing. When we speak about quality of life issues, we often do so in reference to someone who is sick or severely incapacitated. There is a growing liberal sentiment in our country that insists that if we become terminally ill or unable to function normally, it should be our right to end our own life if we so choose. It is offensive to suggest that there is a Creator who alone determines the span of our life. We consider what it would be like to suffer and be unable to escape it. Perhaps we've even witnessed the suffering or incapacitation of someone close to us, and we think, *I don't want to go through that myself, and I don't want to put my loved ones through that. If at all possible, I want to avoid a long illness and a lingering, tortuous death.* These are human and noble feelings.

But there is a dark side to this "quality of life" issue. For example, it has become commonplace to complain that our quality of life is being affected negatively, when what we really mean is that we're in a situation that has made life difficult or inconvenient. "Quality" of life is too often substituted for what is actually "ease" of life.

When it comes to the matters of aging and disabling illness, we do not want to accept some of the conditions life brings to us. We do not like to be confronted with the fact that human capacities can be diminished by age, weakness, limitation, and pain—that makes us face ourselves as the small creatures we really are. We want to see ourselves as masters of our own destiny. We want to believe we can seize the reins of life itself.

THE "QUALITY OF LIFE" ISSUE

Recently, certain medical and genetics researchers have begun to search for the gene that makes us age. The goal of some of these researchers is trumpeted on the recent cover of a publication put out by the Life Extension Foundation in Florida: "Reaching for Immortality." In this issue, Michael D. West, a leading researcher in this field, writes: "In 1997, we . . . succeeded in isolating the gene [that] encodes a protein called *telomerase* that rewinds the clock of aging at the ends of the chromosome. The isolation of this 'immortality gene' stirred considerable controversy as to its potential to 'rewind' the . . . clock in cells in the human body after we showed that it actually works in a laboratory dish. Introducing the gene in an active state literally stops cellular aging. The cells become immortal but are still otherwise normal."

West goes on to explain that there are serious problems with introducing this "immortality gene," created in a lab dish, into the human body. To do so, researchers need to isolate and culture stem cells from the human body, and they must obtain these cells from "human pre-implantation embryos (microscopic balls of cells that have not yet begun to develop and attach to the uterus to begin pregnancies)."

While West and other researchers like him have noble goals that I personally support—to improve the quality of life and reduce the debilitating diseases of aging—the problem is, many in this field have taken it upon themselves to determine when life begins and ends. They have stepped into the role of God. God's plan for human life, which begins at conception and ends at the day and hour He chooses, is a belief many of these researchers reject outright. In the same article, West reflects on the death of his mother, which he says spurred him in this research. He concludes: "As successful as my mother's life might have been in completing the job of reproduction, I [find] the strategy of the life cycle completely unacceptable."

In this way of reasoning, life is reducible to mere biology. Only ongoing biological life equals "success." Far from being the divinely ordered completion of a normal life, the "strategy of the life cycle" that ends in physical death is "completely unacceptable." The concept of an eternal life or a resurrection in which soul and body will be reunited is utterly foreign here. West and others like him have come to believe it is their right, and something of a duty to humanity, to create life in a laboratory dish for the specific purpose of harvesting it on the speculation that it will benefit others. To suggest they are violating the commandment "You shall not murder" is offensive.

Supported by this purely scientific view, insisting that it is our right to have "quality of life," we have become a culture in which life has lost its intrinsic value. If we believe that caring for a child we've conceived is going to stretch us financially or limit our choices, or if that child will be born into a one-parent family, we will insist "quality of life" is the issue. We say things like, "This baby would have been born into poverty and would not have had the benefit of good healthcare and education" or, "This child would not have been born into a loving home, with two parents to care for it." We speak as if it is the *child's* quality of life we're concerned about. If we are honest with ourselves, we know that is not strictly true.

LIFE AND CONVENIENCE

The sad truth is, for the majority of Americans who seek abortion, terminating the life of their unborn child is a matter of personal convenience. Having a child will interfere with their education, their enjoyment of life, their financial goals, or their relationship with a spouse or lover who does not want to care for a child. The decision to end the life of their unborn baby has little or nothing to do with considerations about the *child's* quality of life and everything to do with hopes and plans for their *own*.

The same self-centered attitude generally prevails in our culture when it comes to making decisions about caring for our elderly. Though it is true that some elderly parents need constant monitoring by skilled medical professionals, most really do not. But it seems that fear prevails. In the American mind, it has become a given that caring for an elderly parent is going to demand too much of our time, energy, and financial resources and that it will diminish our quality of life.

Finally, the right to determine "quality of life" has come to encompass the choices we want to make regarding how we desire to end our lives. "I want the right to do what's right for *me*," said a liberal proponent of assisted suicide on a recent national news broadcast. "And I don't want the state or the church telling me I can't end my own life if that's my choice." Clearly, "You shall not murder" is an offense to those who hold this opinion.

All told, the Sixth Commandment affirms that an almighty God is the Creator of life and, therefore, He has ultimate authority over the issues concerning life and death. By extension, God holds the ultimate ownership of our bodies. These concepts are heinous to the liberal mind that holds sway in America, and anyone who supports life is considered oppressive.

Yet the opposite is true. The more we have allowed the liberal line to grant the individual his or her "right" to make the ultimate decisions about life, the cheaper life has become and the more endangered our infants, our elderly, and our sick have become. The more we have valued "quality of life" over life itself, the more lives we have given up to the dark cataclysm of death known as abortion. Spiritually, America has become like the murderous foreign nation, the vision of which horrified the Old Testament prophet Isaiah, causing him to exclaim with dread, "They will have no mercy on infants" (Isaiah 13:18).

How many more lives will be lost in the decades to come if we continue to devalue the lives of the elderly, the sick, and the infirm? How many more deaths will be on our hands if, as a people, we continue to be offended by the words, "You shall not murder?"

THE BLESSINGS OF RESPECTING HUMAN LIFE

It is sad and somewhat disturbing to be at a point in our nation's history where we need to be reminded that honoring and respecting life brings blessing. But there are so many voices telling us life can be chosen or disposed of like a mere commodity, that infants in the womb are "fetal tissue" or "products of conception," and that the elderly, sick, and infirm are an inconvenience, a drain on our "quality of life."

But if we were to obey this commandment, we would find that a godly attitude that honors and respects life does bring blessing.

Not least of all, America as a nation would be blessed.

It is the outpouring of blessing we will experience as a nation when we return to the Lord and obey His command on this crucial matter of life. We need to outlaw the murder of unborn children. We cannot support medical research that conceives life in laboratory dishes, using fertilized human eggs that are only destined to be destroyed. We cannot open the door to assisted suicide.

Human life is of incredible value to the Lord. Life, its beginning and its end, belong to Him. If we return to the Lord on this vastly important matter, our nation will experience a divine favor that God Himself promised:

> All these blessings will come upon you and accompany you if you obey the LORD your God: You will be blessed in the city and blessed in the country. The fruit of your womb will be blessed, and the crops of your land and the young of your livestock. . . . Your basket and your kneading trough will be blessed. You will be blessed when you come in and blessed when you go out. The LORD will grant that the enemies who rise up against you will be defeated before you. . . . The LORD will send a blessing on your barns and everything you put your hand to. The LORD your God will bless you in the land He is giving you. (Deuteronomy 28:2–8)

There is also personal blessing when we obey the Lord by honoring and respecting human life.

On the broadest level, we experience the blessing of safety. "You shall not murder" prevents us from allowing our baser qualities to rule. It places a barrier between us and our wrath, greed, or impulse to seek revenge. It protects us from those who cannot otherwise control their anger. It keeps us safe from those who would kill us to have what we possess. It protects us from those who hate us because of our religion, nationality, income level, or skin color.

"You shall not murder" reminds every one of us that we do not have the right to harm another or take a person's life. That right belongs to One alone, and that is the Lord of life.

Because there is a God who places utmost value on human life, life has meaning. Every single life has purpose.

A DEEPER MEANING TO THIS COMMANDMENT

Jesus Christ plumbed a much deeper meaning for the Sixth Commandment than merely the physical act of murder. He said, "You have heard that it was said to the people long ago, 'Do not murder, and anyone who murders will be subject to judgment.' But I tell you that anyone who is angry with his brother will be subject to judgment. Again, anyone who says to his brother, 'Raca,' is answerable to the Sanhedrin. But anyone who says, 'You fool!' will be in danger of the fire of hell" (Matthew 5:21–22).

Here, according to Jesus, are three nonphysical ways that, knowingly or unknowingly, people break the Sixth Commandment.

First is the violent anger that explodes at another person. We often hear someone say, "I was so mad I could have killed him." The person saying such a thing would probably never dream of completing the act. This is just commonplace expression. But in the spiritual realm, actual violent rage toward another, whether verbalized or silent, is the same as murder. If for no other reason, this explains why parents must teach their children self-discipline. A four-year-old given to temper tantrums may seem harmless, but a grown man still given to temper tantrums becomes a wife beater, a tyrant, and a potential murderer.

Secondly, Jesus said a person is guilty who calls another person "raca." As mentioned in chapter 7, "raca" is an Aramaic word that means its object is worthless and beneath contempt. Our language, especially that of teenagers, is filled with comparables: "airhead," "goof-ball," "jerk," "slimeball," "retard," "geek." Those who write for tele-vision have begun having their characters say repulsive phrases such as, "He is nothing but a worthless piece of [human excrement]."

Each of these terms reduces a human being to something less than human. These epithets cause an individual made in the image of God to become contemptible, without any dignity. According to Jesus Christ, when we apply these terms to someone, we are guilty of murder.

Jesus then warned that those who curse another human being by calling him or her a "fool" would be in danger of the fire of hell. By this, Jesus is not referring to actions that are foolish, but to "the fool" who "says in his heart 'There is no God' " (Psalm 53:1). Such a fool is condemned to hell; therefore, to pronounce such a judgment is not just attempted murder in this life, but in the world to come. Along with this must be added the words that have become far too common on the lips of people today—asking God to "damn" a per-son. By this expression, not only are we taking the Lord's name in vain, we are actually asking God to condemn the object of this out-burst to an eternity in hell.

I am sure someone reading this would say, "But that's just an expression. My friends and I would never intend that meaning." The reality is, that is the meaning of the words, intended or not. Ac-cording to the Bible, people will "have to give account on the day of judgment for every careless word they have spoken. For by your words you will be acquitted, and by your words you will be con-demned" (Matthew 12:36–37).

In His teaching, Jesus did not stop here. He realized that each of us can do or say things to others which cause resentment, rage, or violence. Not only are we to control our own outbursts and de-meaning words, we are to ensure that our actions are not the prov-ocation for someone else's rage toward us. That explains this command: "If you are offering your gift at the altar and then remember that your brother has something against you, leave your gift in front of the altar. First go and be reconciled to your brother, then come and offer your gift" (Matthew 5:23–24).

In short, don't have murder in your words or in your heart toward another, and be sure that your selfish or insensitive actions have not placed murder in someone else's heart toward you!

ENJOYING THE SUPREME GIVER OF LIFE

Our lives are a gift from God. By following God's commands, we can have confidence in spirit, freedom from anxiety, and a deeply abiding peace. We know that our lives lie under the protection and direction of One who is greater than anyone who rises against us or any circumstance that comes to overwhelm us. We can be freed from the empty, rootless wandering that plagues modern, unbelieving mankind. Knowing life is a gift of God frees us from depression and despair. Not only is God our ground of being, He has a purpose for our lives and every incident therein.

Moses recognized that a life lived in obedience to God's commands is rich with blessings when he prayed, "Teach us to number our days aright, that we may gain a heart of wisdom" (Psalm 90:12). He acknowledged that God is the supreme giver of life, and it is He who determines the "span" of our years and the quality of our lives (v. 10).

It was the apostle Peter who said to the Lord Jesus, "Lord, to whom shall we go? You have the words of eternal life" (John 6:68).

As Americans, we need to return to honoring and respecting every life just as we did at the birth of our nation. The right to life still comes before our right to liberty. We must have our eyes opened again to the truth that our lives are in God's hands. My personal prayer is that our nation will turn back to the Lord on every issue where life is concerned. I pray that we will experience all the blessings He will pour out upon us when we put His words of life first, not the demand for personal liberties.

Ten

Commandment Seven: Maintain Sexual Purity

You shall not commit adultery.

—EXODUS 20:14

IN THE BEGINNING, Almighty God said to the first couple, "For this cause a man will leave his father and mother and be united to his wife, and they will become one flesh" (Genesis 2:24).

Our most precious possession is our life. Our second most precious possession is our marriage, because in marriage the spouse actually becomes part of us—one flesh. If someone takes away our spouse, he is literally tearing away part of our being.

I concur with the wisdom of a godly pastor who said, "In the marriage ceremony, we use the term 'till death do us part.' Couples swear before God that their union will remain until death. Therefore, when divorce takes place, a death takes place along with it. By solemn oath, they have agreed that their parting can only be by death. So if they voluntarily end their union, that which they have sworn before God will take place—part of them will die."

In the book of Genesis, we find the story of the sojourning of Abraham, the great patriarch, with his wife, Sarah, who was an extraordinarily beautiful woman. In one instance, we learn that Abraham believed that Abimelech, the king of the region, would kill him in order to take his wife away from him. Since he and Sarah had the same father but different mothers, he instructed her to tell Abimelech that she was his sister. Upon hearing that, Abimelech took Sarah into his household to be part of his harem.

The Bible tells us that before there was any sexual contact between Abimelech and Sarah, God came to Abimelech in a dream and said:

> "You are a dead man, for that woman you took is married." But Abimelech had not slept with her yet, so he said, "Lord, will you kill an innocent man? Abraham told me, 'She is my sister,' and she herself said, 'Yes, he is my brother.' I acted in complete innocence!"
>
> "Yes, I know you are innocent," God replied. . . . "Now return her to her husband . . . but if you don't return her to him, you can be sure that you and your entire household will die." . . .
>
> Then Abimelech called for Abraham. "What is this you have done to us," he demanded, ". . . making *me and my kingdom guilty of this great sin?*" . . . For the Lord had stricken all the women with infertility as a warning to Abimelech for having taken Abraham's wife . . . (See Genesis 20.)

Consider the penalty of adultery in this account. God was prepared to kill a king and his entire household if he committed adultery with the wife of God's prophet. The consequence of adultery was not only death, but infertility to all the women until Sarah was restored to her husband. This so-called heathen king recognized adultery as a "great sin."

AMERICA'S VIEW OF ADULTERY

There is an incredible disconnect between a God who is prepared to strike a king dead for attempting to have sex with another man's wife, and the current blasé attitude of modern-day America that perceives sex outside of marriage as no big deal.

A recently released Barna survey shows that over 40 percent of the people in America see nothing "morally" wrong with sexual dalliances by married men and women with people of the opposite sex who are not their mates. The cover story in a recent issue of *Business Week* boldly proclaimed "Unmarried America" and described the alarming trend toward couples living together apart from marriage.

Young adults don't talk of marriage; they talk of entering a "relationship" or "hooking up." They cohabitate with one another, they have sex with one another, and if the relationship doesn't work, they pick one of the "fifty ways to leave your lover" and take a hiatus. Then, after a few months, they begin another relationship, and so the cycle continues.

The formality of marriage is avoided or postponed for years. At the 2000 U.S. Census, there were 5.5 million couples living together outside of marriage, and the trend is accelerating. Tragically for the nation, for every two new marriages that take place in America, one marriage ends in divorce—a 50 percent divorce rate. From the viewpoint of the Ten Commandments, this coupling and uncoupling is tantamount to the nationwide practice of adultery.

AMERICA'S DECLINE INTO ADULTERY

There was a time not long ago that the Christian view of sexuality prevailed. Sure, there was kissing and petting between young couples. Yes, young men were considered predators, but young men and women were taught that sexual intercourse was for marriage, and sex outside of marriage was sin. I can remember clearly the college days after World War II. Young women were not as widely promiscuous in America in those days, and even predatory single males were horrified that their married schoolmates would consider cheating on their spouses. Even the wildest fraternity crowd did not condone adultery.

Then Margaret Sanger, the founder of Planned Parenthood, desired to introduce eugenics to America by sterilization of the unfit. To that end, she apparently believed the most effective way to win public support for sterilization would be to have teenagers engaging in unbridled sex and getting pregnant out of wedlock. Her campaign gained powerful financial support, including huge taxpayer-funded government subsidies.

Along with the campaign of Planned Parenthood was the much-heralded Kinsey Report on American sexuality. Kinsey's supposedly scientific findings portrayed Americans as much more free from sexual restraint than we had ever believed. Kinsey seemed to give credence to those who wanted sexual expression with no restraint. There was only one problem. Later information about Kinsey's work revealed that his "typical Americans" included inmates in prison who were convicted sex offenders and prostitutes. Some children in the study actually sobbed and cried as they were experimented upon sexually. And Kinsey himself, it turns out, was a bisexual and suspected pedophile. These discoveries came too late. The damage was done by his widely heralded "scientific" findings.

In the 1960s and 1970s, a woman named Mary Calderone and an organization called the Sexuality Information and Education Council of the US (SIECUS) began an all-out drive to introduce sex education into public schools. This curriculum, and others like it, showed none of the spiritual aspects of human reproduction or the Christian concept of sexual restraint before marriage. SIECUS began to impose on teenagers and younger children a thoroughly secular and amoral view of human anatomy and sexual relations.

A few years ago I glanced at a teachers' handbook for a local high school. The pictures were so explicit they would be banned on network television. But this was the educators' view of what should be taught to teenagers.

Is there any wonder that by the twenty-first century, more and more people in America came to view nothing "immoral" about sexual relations between unmarried people living together or sexual experience outside of marriage?

Listen to the warning in Proverbs: "Wisdom will save you from the immoral woman, from the flattery of the adulterous woman. She has abandoned her husband and ignores the covenant she made before God. Entering her house leads to death; it is the road to hell. The man who visits her is doomed. He will never reach the paths of life" (Proverbs 2:16–18 NLT).

These words are serious. It is clear that God takes marriage very seriously and He will go to extraordinary lengths to defend it and to punish those who defile it.

WHY IS MARRIAGE IMPORTANT?

Marriage is important for several reasons, but for our purposes here, let me focus on only two. First of all, marriage is God's chosen mechanism to bring forth life created in His image. God made the sex act enjoyable so that married couples would have an incentive to procreate and, therefore, sustain the human race.

Secondly, marriage is important because marriage is essential for the care and nurture of the young. Children growing up need a nurturing mother and a caring father. There are dozens of psychological and sociological studies that reveal the damage done to young children raised without a father—lack of drive, inattention, poor grades, unsocial behavior, and susceptibility to drugs. Although there are notable exceptions, the crucial role of a caring father in the development of boys and girls is not open to dispute.

As I have shown in chapter 9, the family unit is the essential building block of society. Towns and villages, cities, states, and nations are built upon families. If the family unit is strong, society is strong. If families lack cohesion, society will ultimately collapse.

THE CONSEQUENCES OF ADULTERY

The average man works to support himself and his family. He wants to provide food, shelter, and clothing for his wife and his children. He will work long hours so that his children will have proper medical care, recreational advantages, a well-rounded education, and a good start in life. This may sound old-fashioned, but it is true.

He does these things as long as his vital energies are centered in his home. Once he begins one or more adulterous affairs, his life becomes a lie. He must hide his conduct from his wife and his children. He loses focus. His work suffers. His wife quickly notices that her husband's attention to her is not open and loving, but perfunctory and mechanical. She feels neglected and hurt, so she lashes back. The situation worsens as the children find themselves in the midst of a bitter struggle, and the wife fears being infected with a potentially life-threatening sexual disease brought home by her philandering husband.

In this case, the price of adultery is damage to the husband's future, damage to the wife, damage to the children, damage to the husband's employer, and damage to the civic, moral, and financial health of the community.

Consider the consequences of a wife's adultery. There is the same hurt, sense of rejection, family feud, possibility of sexually transmitted disease, marital breakup, damage to children, and damage to society. But what is the attitude of a father who learns that the child or children for whom he is working so hard to provide a future were actually sired by his wife's lover? What about inheritance—the family home, the family farm, the family business, the costly insurance policies? The damage of a sexual dalliance outside of marriage can bring about consequences to two individuals that sometimes cannot be calculated.

Is it any wonder that a loving God says, "I hate divorce" (Malachi 2:16), and to those He would protect from one of life's greatest tragedies, "You shall not commit adultery" (Exodus 20:14)?

WHAT IS ADULTERY?

Adultery is sexual intercourse by either husband or wife outside of marriage. The term *fornication*, which the apostle Paul describes in 1 Corinthians 6:18 as a sin "against [your] own body," is sexual intercourse between two unmarried people.

Jesus Christ raised the concept of adultery from the purely physical sex act to an act of the mind. He said that "anyone who looks at a woman lustfully has already committed adultery with her in his heart" (Matthew 5:28). To Jesus, engaging in a sexual act in the heart is tantamount to doing so with the body. In short, if a married man were engaging in sexual fantasies with a woman in his heart, he would undoubtedly follow through physically if given a chance. Since we are spiritual beings for eternity and physical beings for only a few years, what is done in the spirit has much more profound consequences before God than what we do physically.

According to one of his former girlfriends, the former president of the United States Bill Clinton was a sex addict who could not keep his hands off women. Somewhere along the way, Clinton had convinced himself that oral sex and telephone sex were not adultery. The Paula Jones lawsuit involved his alleged attempt, while governor, to have an unknown state employee perform oral sex on him. The Monica Lewinski episode involved a young White House intern allegedly being asked to perform repeated acts of oral sex on him in a room adjoining the Oval Office. Evidently Clinton's mind was so deluded that he believed this was not sex or adultery. He declared before the American people, "I did not have sex with that woman, Miss Lewinski."

Remember, all this time Bill Clinton was married to Hillary Rodham Clinton, and they had a child by that marriage. Yet a large number of Americans do not believe that his sexual conduct was morally wrong.

INTERNET ADULTERY

Perhaps Clinton is indicative of our times. In 2003 there are 167,000 Internet sites that mention sex, 39,000 listed as XXX, plus 57,000 listed as pornographic. These websites make up the most lucrative facet of the Internet, as pornography has become a multi-billion-dollar enterprise.

A quick scan of the table of contents of some of these purveyors of filth reveals subject matter that would shock the sensibility of all but the totally depraved. In times past, only a tiny fraction of our population would ever consider frequenting tawdry peep shows. Now portrayals of unimaginable sexual acts are available in the privacy of one's home. In order to hook the unwary, pornographers have claimed every imaginable Internet address, such as "Little-Women" and "WhiteHouse.com."

Our CBN News researchers discovered scientific evidence that pornography is as addictive as cocaine or heroin, going directly to the pleasure centers of the brain. This addiction is so powerful that thousands of reports from heartbroken women give testimony to the fact that their husbands, when offered a choice or an ultimatum, will take the voluptuous fantasy world of pornography and cybersex over real life and real intimacy with their spouse.

The numbers may be artificially high, but several sources say that an estimated 45 percent of the adult population has used some form of pornography. With the cruder forms of pornography comes a lowering of the standards for cable television and then broadcast television. First it is a quick peep at a topless dancer, then pictures of lap dancing, followed by full frontal nudity, and then graphic displays of intercourse. But it doesn't stop there. Soon it is followed by homosexual acts and then such things as bestiality, child pornography, graphic rape scenes, sadomasochism, and so-called snuff films where the victim either pretends to be killed or is actually killed.

Married men and women who indulge in these kinds of fantasies are breaking God's holy commandment forbidding adultery. Adultery is sweeping our society, yet the commandment is no longer considered a blessing but an offense.

When concerned Americans attempt to raise a standard in support of the Seventh Commandment and biblical morality, they are accused of violating the "First Amendment rights" of the pornographers. Those who cry out against the abuses are ridiculed, demeaned, and shouted down by those who do not want any restraint whatsoever on sexual practices or on the public depiction of them. They hide behind the First Amendment to the Constitution, which they use to remove our public affirmation of religious faith, while at the same time claiming its protection for unbridled sexual expression.

THE OFFENSE OF THE SEVENTH COMMANDMENT

More and more, any call for sexual purity is seen as a puritanical restriction on freedom of expression and a laughable "offense."

I will never forget the experience I had in the 1960s when the Phi Beta Kappa chapter at the College of William and Mary held a debate about the role of law and pornography. On the other side was the movie critic of the *New York Daily News* and Russ Meyer, a veteran producer and director of pornographic films. Meyer and his cohorts were arguing that artists should be allowed artistic expression so that they could produce "high-quality, big-budget motion pictures."

Of course, everything they said was a bald-faced lie, but the coeds in the audience supported every word. These young girls refused to affirm the clear premise that pornography is a massive attempt to demean and exploit women sexually.

Case in point: I later learned that the "big-budget art film" *Deep Throat* had actually cost $25,000 to produce, yet it grossed a staggering $145 million (adjusted for inflation) in America alone. I also learned that the female star (or victim), whose stage name was Linda Lovelace, had been paid only $200 per week for her appalling performance. I also learned that she was married to one of the principals in the company, who reportedly had beaten and drugged her to force her to perform disgusting acts on film. Finally, I learned that her mother was a fundamentalist Christian who learned of the way her daughter was being mistreated but told her that it was "God's will that she submit to her husband." What an utter distortion of Christian doctrine.

So much for the "big-budget expression of art" protected by the First Amendment. My argument in this debate was simple. Liberals exert every effort to remove pollution from our air and our water. Why should we not be allowed to remove harmful pollution from our films and television? One day we may wake up to the harm this noxious poison is doing throughout our society, but so far the pornographers, aided by the courts, appear to be winning.

THE BLESSING OF THE SEVENTH COMMANDMENT

Leaving aside the corrosive effect that breaking the Seventh Commandment has on our society, consider the blessing of keeping it.

Think of the peace of mind that comes to a woman who can say, "My husband has chosen me as his only partner and companion for life. He loves and cherishes me, and I can rely on his faithfulness to me." Or to the husband who can say, "My wife has chosen me as her husband for life. Together we will build a home, raise our children, and labor together for the mutual good of our family. I love her and she loves me, and neither of us will give ourselves to any other."

That marriage is built on trust, not jealousy and suspicion. God's commandment gives complete peace of mind that each partner can be secure in the marriage—the most precious of possessions other than life itself. Husband and wife build on a secure foundation. Their children never have to face the tragic consequences of a broken home. And they, in turn, have an example to follow when they marry and build a secure home of their own. The Psalmist put it beautifully:

> How happy are those who fear the LORD—
> All who follow his ways!
> You will enjoy the fruit of your labor.
> How happy you will be! How rich your life!
> Your wife will be like a fruitful vine,
> Flourishing within your home.
> And look at all those children!
> There they sit around your table
> As vigorous and healthy as young olive trees.
> This is Jehovah's reward
> For those who fear him. (Psalm 128:1–4 NLT)

Fidelity is a word we do not hear much today. It means faithful devotion and loyalty. If we obey the Seventh Commandment, we will experience the blessings that come from faithful devotion and from receiving loyalty from another.

First, fidelity to another allows us to experience personal blessings that far outweigh the fleeting pleasures found when we make personal pleasure our god. This is not to say that marriage is easy. It isn't. Marriage is a lifelong commitment to grow with and to deeply engage another human being who is, like us, flawed. So it is fraught with struggle and effort. Here we need someone to see us just as we are, to accept us and forgive us, and to encourage the best from us. We are blessed with this challenge to grow and to overcome personal flaws and weaknesses and become better human beings.

Of course, beyond this are other blessings that come with keeping a lifelong commitment to another. We experience the emotional benefits of a shared history, which give roots and stability to our souls. We feel the deep, settled feeling that comes with knowing we belong somewhere and belong with someone. We know we are not alone in the world, but there is someone who cares for us. Someone—a wife, a husband, children—waits for us to come home.

The emotional blessing that comes with fidelity includes comfort and strength for the hard times. Most of us marry at a time in life when we are youthful, hopeful, healthy, and when visions of a bright future lie ahead. But life is full of darker moments and hardship. We need the blessing of fidelity for the day when a doctor gives us terrifying news or the day our career comes to a dead-end. As surely as we need someone to share life's great and bright moments, we need someone at our side to walk with us through loss, grief, depression, and despair until better days return.

A BLESSING IN SPIRIT

Obeying the Seventh Commandment holds yet another blessing—a blessing in spirit. The moment we pledge fidelity to another, we destine ourselves to encounter every temptation to our loyalty and every weak spot in the walls of our morality. If we are honest with ourselves, we come to know ourselves and our human weakness intimately. Knowing that in our own strength we would fail, however, we learn to throw ourselves upon the mercy of God and depend upon His strength. As a result, we experience the blessing of greater fellowship with God and more resilience in spirit.

Only after he fell into adultery did David learn to pray, "Search me, O God, and know my heart. . . . See if there is any offensive way in me" (Psalm 139:23–24). David welcomed the searchlight of God's Spirit, even begging Him to expose the lustful thoughts and weak places in his soul. Through the painful and devastating aftermath of his sin with Bathsheba, David learned that allowing God to expose the roots of temptation is the only way to prevent them from growing and coming to destructive fruition as sin. Along with that knowledge, David discovered the blessing of a deeper, stronger, truer relationship with his soul's Creator. It was through this relationship that David the adulterer became a man of character.

As a nation we are being slowly eaten away from within by adultery. This is no wonder, because the spirit that drives adultery is a hungry, dissatisfied spirit.

And yet God's blessing can still be ours . . . *if* we will turn away from the spirit of this age and ask the Lord to strengthen us from within. Where we are weak, God Himself is constant. His love and faithfulness endure forever (Psalm 136).

At this hour in our nation's history, with sexual corruption at its highest level ever, we need God to restore purity to our land. I pray that this commitment to purity remains strong in my heart and in the hearts of men and women throughout America—all of those who long for blessing to replace blight in our nation.

ELEVEN

Commandment Eight: Respect Others' Property

You shall not steal.

—EXODUS 20:15

Edward Stern is one of the wealthiest men in America and the founder of Canary Capital Partners, a highly successful investment firm. He is also the latest in a string of American financial moguls to be found guilty of illegal practices, essentially robbing competitors of their advantage in the marketplace by unethical trading practices. He very nearly got away with $30 million in illegal gains.

What makes cases like Stern's so interesting is that the man engineering the scheme is a person of wealth—staggering wealth, really.

A writer for the *New York Times* describes Stern as a member of "the eleventh richest family in New York City." He is heir to a fortune amassed by his grandfather, Max Stern, who founded the Hartz Mountain pet supplies company and who further increased his family fortune by leasing warehouse space to other companies, leaving his family with wealth in excess of $3 billion. Being heir to a fortune and all of the privileges it bought, including a penthouse on Central Park West, was just not enough for Edward Stern.

When the Bank of America came courting, wanting Stern to

bank Canary Capital monies with it, he saw an opportunity. He would work with Bank of America in exchange for a favor—the ability to move money rapidly into and out of various mutual funds. This practice, known as market timing, is not illegal or unethical in and of itself. But there was something else.

Stern insisted that the traders at his firm have access to a bank computer that allowed them to keep trading mutual fund shares for hours after the market's 4:00 P.M. cutoff time. Wanting access to all the new capital, Bank of America agreed. They were not the only institution drawn in by Stern's scheme. He also struck a deal with Security Trust Company, a Phoenix firm that allowed Canary Capital access to its computers for after-market trading up until 9:00 P.M.

What made these deals unethical was that they allowed Stern to act on financial information released after Wall Street's closing bell. If late-day financial information told him a stock held by a fund would drop in price when the market opened the following morning, he could sell at today's higher price. If news told him a stock would gain, he would invest in the mutual fund's shares at today's lower closing cost. Other investors had to wait, of course, until the next day to make their trades. With this unfair advantage fueling their "predictions," Canary Capital appeared to have uncanny acumen. That aura of financial "genius" lured more and more high-roller investors, driving the firm's investment dollars up to a high-water mark of some $730 million in assets.

Stern was not really a success—not unless you equate robbing your way to the top of the financial investing heap as successful. He almost got away with these dishonest trading tactics, allowing him to realize tremendous profits at the expense of other mutual-fund investors.

That Stern did not actually steal money is a fact that kept him out of federal prison. Without admitting any thievery, he agreed to pay back $30 million in restitution to investors.

I use the word *thievery* nonetheless because Stern engaged in thefts of a different kind. By finding a way to cheat the investment system, he stole clients away from other investment firms—companies that play by the rules. After gaining their confidence, he then robbed those investors of earnings their money might have made them had it been invested by honest means. They were paid back what they invested, but any potential gain on that money was lost.

Yet Stern is not alone. In fact, his actions were penny ante compared to the big corporate scandals of the past couple of years. The Rigas family is accused of looting in excess of $2 billion from a public company they founded and controlled, Adelphia Communications. Dennis Kozlowski and his associates are under indictment for allegedly enriching themselves at the expense of Tyco. The press has been full of the sordid details of a lifestyle worthy of a king—$6,000 shower curtains, a $15,000 umbrella stand, apartment furnishings pegged at $12 million, multimillion-dollar paintings, a costly yacht as well as a lavish residence in Florida. Richard Scrushy, founder and head of HealthSouth, has been charged in an eighty-five-count indictment with fraudulently inflating earnings of this public company while enriching himself by "several hundred million dollars."

Then there is the story of Sunday school teacher Bernie Ebbers, whose WorldCom, after taking over telephone giant MCI, is alleged to have perpetrated the largest bookkeeping fraud in corporate history. And, of course, there is Enron, whose chief financial officer, Andrew Fastow, established a series of off-balance-sheet partnerships to hide debt and make Enron's statements to lenders and investors appear better than they actually were. Enron practiced further deceit on investors by round-robin sales of power in order to make its gross revenues much larger than honest accounting would have permitted.

Now under investigation for market timing of mutual funds are people from such trusted names as Putnam, Janus, and Strong. Together, all of the shady dealings in mutual funds probably cost unsophisticated and trusting small investors several billion dollars in the market value of their mutual-fund shares. And, in the case of WorldCom and Enron, their demise resulted in virtually the total loss of the money that had been invested in their common stock— all because of greed, lies, and theft of value.

VARIOUS WAYS TO STEAL

Taking what belongs to someone else is not the only way to steal. Yes, most major American cities are plagued with burglaries and armed robberies. Major retailers report that shoplifters walk off with $10–12 billion in stolen merchandise each year. Businesses complain that stealing by their employees, through embezzlement by white-collar workers and petty thefts by lower-ranking employees, costs them astronomical losses in both cash and equipment.

To give just one example, I believe stealing at restaurants by employees has reached a fine art. One hotel with which I am familiar was losing large sums of money on its popular food service. It became obvious that rampant theft by the food staff was taking place. So security guards were secretly introduced into the kitchen staff to observe. What they found was appalling. Boxes of frozen steaks, chicken, beef patties, whole roasts, hams, and turkeys were being sent out in the garbage and later picked up by the thieves. Silver serving dishes, plates, and other utensils were going the same way. When the ring of thieves was identified and fired, the hotel restaurant became profitable. The remaining staff realized that secret operatives were watching them and that crime for them would not pay.

A friend of mine in the Midwest owns what is reported to be the most profitable MacDonald's franchise in America. Faced with theft of food and money, he instituted stringent controls. At the beginning and end of each day, he counted everything that could result in daily income—plastic tops, glasses, containers, everything. If the tally did not square, the person responsible was fired. As I recall, he told me the average gross profit at comparable restaurants without theft controls is 11 percent. His gross profit is 30 percent. What a sorry indictment on the honesty of American workers who choose at will to ignore the Eighth Commandment.

Kids steal millions of dollars from recording artists and their companies by downloading music via the Internet. Cable television companies lose millions to adults who hook into their services without paying. These types of theft are a bad enough plague in our society, but in America, outright stealing is not the only way we violate the Eighth Commandment. We keep coming up with newer kinds of stealing all the time.

• *We steal by defaulting on loans.* Credit-card default costs lending companies more each year as Americans fail to cover debts for goods and services they never had money to pay for in the first place. Many who do this do not run up just one credit card to the maximum amount before defaulting; they do it with two or three cards before they are stopped. Some are forced into bankruptcy. As a result, credit-card companies are forced to increase interest rates, passing the loss on to those of us who pay our bills regularly and on time. We are the ones whose pockets are picked by credit deadbeats.

• *We steal "accomplishment."* In many U.S. colleges and universities, students and professors are now working in collusion, pumping up grade-point averages for a price. "Grade fraud," or giving a student his actual grade in class while posting a higher grade on his permanent record, has become a shockingly common practice. Creating the appearance of high achievement, graduates defraud potential employers. In essence, they wind up stealing positions in the workforce that they haven't earned by real accomplishment.

• *We steal power.* In 2003, Jason Blair, one of the leading and most powerful reporters for the *New York Times,* was found to be creating "facts" to support his investigative news stories. Yes, he was lying, but he was lying for the purpose of gaining a better position and more power at the *Times*. What he did is not unlike what many American politicians do all the time, playing to the popular vote during their campaigns with the real intention of benefiting their wealthy supporters once elected. Such men and women essentially steal power for their own use.

• *We steal identities.* At an ever-quickening pace, identity theft is becoming a serious problem in America. We are no longer safe to use our credit cards, our Social Security numbers, or to give out any kind of personal information. A new breed of thief is stealing identities and using for criminal purposes the good names we have worked hard to build. The damage caused to their victims includes years of hardship as they try to undo the mess done to their credit and to remove the stain from their once-good name.

• *We steal wages.* There was a time in America when the slogan "An honest day for an honest dollar" was the accepted norm for those who received wages. For many these days, such a concept is a joke. People report to work and immediately begin to eat their breakfast on company time. Hours are stolen from employers through wasted gossip at the water cooler, talking on the phone with family and friends, reviewing personal stock portfolios, or worse still, using the company Internet connection to view pornography. Since the law mandates time-and-a-half salary for overtime, it is easy for a worker who is not closely supervised to boost his or her pay by hanging around the office or factory for extra hours doing unnecessary busywork so he or she can claim overtime. And on top of stealing wages for work not really performed, there are false claims for reimbursement of expenses that never took place. If outside workers and their supervisors are in collusion, they can steal their employers blind with fraudulent expense accounts and overtime claims.

Stealing *in kind* is stealing nonetheless. In reality, it is another of the subtle ways that we in America violate the Ten Commandments. But then, to many of us, God's prohibition against stealing is just another law that seems to grate on our souls.

WHY IS STEALING SO POPULAR?

Of the crimes committed against individuals in America, stealing is in a slight decline as I write. In 1999 armed robberies totaled just under 700,000. In 2001 home burglaries numbered over 3.1 million, and incidents of larceny, from petty stealing to grand theft, totaled more than 8.1 million at their highest level. That means almost 12 million Americans were victimized each year by some form of stealing.

How can we begin to account for such rampant crime? There are those who would point to social conditions. There is, in fact, a widening gap between those who are struggling economically and those who are doing well. There are more single-parent homes, where young people have little guidance. Drug dealing and fencing stolen merchandise are easy ways to make money, and they beckon to our children, especially those in poor families. But "want" and "need" are not the only contributing factors. We have been infected, I believe, by a cultural mind-set that feeds lawlessness and the belief that it is, in fact, all right to steal.

America under the influence of today's liberal thinking is about *entitlement*. Whereas the biblical world-view on which our country was founded promotes diligence and work as the road to success, we have become a nation of people who believe we should have that for which we have not worked. The "American Dream" was once founded on a principle: Hard work will get you what you want. Today that dream has transformed into an illusion, a form of mental derangement. We think that because we live in the wealthiest nation on earth, someone should give us what we want regardless of the quality of our work or the level of our achievement.

At the same time, the liberal view of man promoted by most

secular psychologists today promotes the idea that stealing is not so much a crime as it is evidence that thieves are, themselves, only victims. Stealing does not mean we are morally flawed, they say; it means that our parents or teachers did not give us what we need or that society has denied us something. We do not need a God telling us what to do; we need therapy. As Alan Wolfe noted in *The Transformation of American Religion,* even Christian ministers often dip more heavily into psychological jargon than they do the Scriptures. "Sinful acts are explained away, as preachers invoke . . . diagnostic disorders assembled by the American Psychological Association. . . . Rare is the sermon that dwells on sin if doing so leaves a gloomy message."

We do not want to call stealing sin, and we surely do not want to call a thief a thief.

THE SOURCE OF OUR DISCONTENT

While Americans have been shifting to this morally neutral view of human behavior, we are a nation of people who have the highest standard of living on earth, and yet we are not content. This is because a constant parade of wondrous new products is trotted before our eyes on television, in catalogs, and in advertisements. Advertisers practice a craft known as "creative strategic discontent," which means they know exactly how to convey the message, "You must have *this* if you want to feel good, and feel good about yourself." If American society can be classified, it is most definitely a "feel-good" society.

If we take a step back, we see how two attitudes combine in the American soul, creating a toxic effect: We *need* things—things make us *feel* we're okay; and, because we're Americans, we *should* be able to have what we want, no matter how we get it. We have believed it is our right to determine our own material destiny and find our way to such fortune as we can amass in this lifetime. It is at this point that God's law becomes extremely troublesome.

Of course, the Eighth Commandment stands against all shop-lifters, petty larcenists, burglars, and armed robbers. It stands in the way of the rank thief, whether the kid who steals for fun or the career criminal with a string of robberies on his rap sheet. It also bores more deeply, exposing an unpleasant side of our American idea of self-determinism.

"You shall not steal" chafes against our sense that we *must have* whatever it is we want. On one hand, God's law opposes our belief that material gain or achieving rank or status will make us happy. Many people truly believe that "he who dies with the most toys wins." On the other hand, it opposes our will and sets a barrier in our way when we say to ourselves, "Even if every honest way of getting what I want fails, one road is still open to me. I'll just take what I want. After all, I *need* it." Who is God to tell us we can't just take what will make us happy? "You shall not steal" reminds us that our will to possess can have a damaging and evil side unless it is under the control of God's law.

Parallel to this, the Eighth Commandment rubs raw the American spirit of entitlement. We have been programmed by liberal rhetoric to believe that we should have that which we have not earned or achieved through real effort. Today, any voice that opposes social and economic programs handing out money, services not earned, or benefits not based on actual need, is an enemy. We have only to consider the welfare fraud so rampant today, and we realize the immense crime being perpetrated against those in real need of this protective net and against the working people who support this system with their tax dollars. Every truly needy person in America ought to be able to find help and not hit bottom. But in America, the spirit of entitlement perversely climbs up the social ladder, creating the attitude: "If other people are getting theirs, I should get mine," whether or not we deserve it, whether or not we can earn it.

THE POLITICS OF ENTITLEMENT

Karl Marx established a society based on greed, envy, and plunder. "From each according to his ability—to each according to his need," had a lovely biblical sound to it. In truth, it was no such thing.

In the time of the early church, people who had houses and land sold them and voluntarily gave the proceeds to the apostles to distribute to the poor. A man named Ananias sold some land, held back a portion, and then tried to make believe that he and his wife were giving everything in the same fashion as the others. The apostle Peter certainly opposed the premise of communism when he said, "Ananias, the *property was yours* to sell or not sell, as you wished. And after selling it, the *money was yours* to give away" (Acts 5:4–5; emphasis added). There was no force, no rule, no requirement by God that the early Christian people give up their property for the needy. "The property was yours . . . the money was yours."

However, Marxism was different. The people who made up the early Bolshevik or Communist Party had few material possessions, so they forcibly seized the property of those who had possessions. They seized farms, factories, houses, livestock, machinery, bank accounts—everything. All supposedly went to the state, but in point of fact it provided a life of comfort and luxury for the new ruling class. Whatever the rationale, this was state-sponsored theft, pure and simple.

The steeply graduated income tax and the inheritance tax were both the creation of Marxist communism, which was based on class warfare—the proletariat versus the aristocracy and the bourgeois.

In today's America, we hear every major Democratic presidential candidate beating the drum for class warfare. Despite the disturbing disparity of wealth that exists in America, the simple truth is that the bottom 25 percent of income earners pay scarcely any income tax at all. The top 1 percent pay 34 percent of all taxes, the top 5 percent pay 53 percent, the top 25 percent of income earners pay

83 percent of all taxes, and the top 50 percent pay 96 percent of all taxes! The bottom 50 percent of wage earners shoulder only 4 percent of the total tax burden.

Yet the politics of envy say that government should confiscate even more of the earning power of the productive sector of society so that there can be more money for the bureaucrats to spend. I am hardly an apostle of unrestrained greed and lavish living in the midst of grinding poverty. People of wealth have a positive duty to give generously to the work of the Lord and to those who are less fortunate in society. The word of Jesus Christ in this regard is clear: "From everyone who has been given much, much will be demanded" (Luke 12:48). All of us hold our earthly possessions as life stewards. We came into this world with nothing material, and we will leave it with nothing material.

In the Old Testament Law of Moses was the concept of the Jubilee. Assets based on loans to others could be accumulated for forty-nine years. The means of production of agricultural products could be accumulated for forty-nine years. But at the end of forty-nine years, during the fiftieth year, like a giant *Monopoly* game, all the debts were canceled, the land reverted to its original tribe, all slaves were freed, and the game began again. During the half-century, a person could play the money game in accordance with God's laws as hard as he wished. At the end of the period, a new set of players could try their skill.

At no time did the government step in and penalize a man for his success. God ordained tithes and offerings. No more. The government was to allow the people to enjoy what God had given them, not try to take it away.

The Fourth Amendment in the United States Constitution states in part, "The rights of the people to be secure in their persons, houses, papers, and effects against unreasonable searches and seizure, shall not be violated."

In the United States today, any person of means lives in fear of rapacious lawyers. He is not "secure in [his] houses, papers, and effects." It may have the appearance of legality, but the tort bar has organized judicial theft to a fine art. Virtually anyone in America who has any possessions at all can find himself or herself the subject of a genuine or spurious lawsuit that could result in the plaintiff and his lawyer taking everything they have. Seminars are held to teach people to have peace of mind from rapacious thieves by organizing trusts in foreign jurisdictions, offshore corporations, spousal transfers, and family partnerships.

The fear generated by these purveyors of "peace of mind" is to some degree contrived, but the fear I have seen in South America is not.

In the late 1960s, CBN purchased a radio station, Emisora Nuevo Continente, in Bogotá, Columbia. I traveled to Bogotá somewhat frequently. In that city, people regularly removed the windshield wipers from their cars or they would have been stolen. At the end of the day, shopkeepers pulled a heavy metal shield in front of their store windows and bolted it to the sidewalk to prevent thieves from breaking the glass in front of their shops and stealing their goods. A high wall topped by broken bottles, concertina wire, or both, surrounded houses in the wealthier districts, not only in Bogotá, but San Salvador, Mexico City, Rio de Janeiro, and São Paolo. Automobiles were brought off the street inside an area that was secure and locked. Many people hired armed security guards to protect their property and to prevent kidnapping for ransom of themselves or their family members.

Despite these precautions, there were many robberies, murders, and kidnappings. In these places, everyone lives in a measure of fear. How can there be peace and happiness if someone is always there to steal from you?

I was told that the early Presbyterian missionaries to Jamaica had such a profound effect in the early days that the people were strong believers in the Law of Jehovah. They were so averse to stealing that no defense against it was thought necessary. If a person left his home for a period of time, he merely placed a stick diagonally across his doorframe to show that he was not there. The commandment of God stood guard—nothing else was needed.

By prohibiting us from stealing, God points us in the direction of work. Honest hard work, sometimes even toil, will get our "wants" and "needs" met. America, a land of golden promise, is the nation where dreams are supposed to come true. But the Eighth Commandment is a reminder that, since the Fall of man in the Garden of Eden, work is our lot. The apostle Paul told the early Christians, "He who has been stealing must steal no longer, but must work, doing something useful with his own hands" (Ephesians 4:28). Though Christ has opened the doors to heaven of eternal bliss by His sacrifice, here on earth we are to rise each morning and set out to earn our livelihoods "by the sweat of [our] brow" (Genesis 3:19).

THE BLESSINGS OF THE EIGHTH COMMANDMENT

As much as I believe "You shall not steal" is a reminder that sinful man is always looking to obtain something that he has not earned, I believe it is a commandment rich with blessing too.

At its simplest level, of course, the Eighth Commandment protects what belongs to us. It has found its way into our Constitution and stands among the founding truths of our nation as the right to own property. It is because the God who loves us prohibits others from taking what we've worked to earn that thieves can be prosecuted.

Even our ideas can be protected by copyrights, patents, and trademarks. Every time someone creates an enterprise like Napster, where creative properties can be stolen and income picked from the pockets of artists, God's Eighth Commandment is there to shield from loss by theft. As a side note, it seems especially poignant, if not ironic, that many recording artists today who openly oppose God's laws and mock traditional morality rely on His law to protect them when their property rights are at stake.

The blessing of this commandment does not stop with our personal protection. "You shall not steal" extends its wall of defense to our families as well. What is gifted to us through the generosity of our forebears enjoys protection under our laws. No one has the right to seize the inheritance we receive, nor do they have the right to take away the estate we leave for our children and grandchildren. With God's law instructing us to work for honest gain, we teach our children that it is right and good to earn their way in life. Training them in this way, we help them to enjoy the blessings of good self-esteem that come as they are rewarded for honest effort and achievement.

Without God's law to intervene, it is human nature to take what we want, even if it belongs to someone else. To the soul apart from God, real loss to another human being does not matter much. What counts is getting what we want.

Beneath our impulse to steal, there lies a deeper root. As a race, we seem to carry an almost universal wish to have all that we need or want given to us—a latent resentment, even anger, that it is our lot to work. We suffer from our longings and do not really like that, in our fall from grace, we have brought so much toil upon ourselves. Apart from God, our work has become meaningless toil to be merely endured. In our drive to possess more, we work more hours than almost any other nation on earth, and we have more wealth per capita than any other people on earth. Yet we are not content.

Those of us who know the love of God, however, see that the Eighth Commandment offers great blessings to us and our nation. Whatever our hand finds to do, we do it with all our might because we labor with joy as unto the Lord (Ecclesiastes 9:10; Colossians 3:23). To the Christian, work becomes divine service, not a hardship. We do not take what isn't ours; we set our hands to do meaningful work.

As America suffers from an increasing lawlessness, let us pray that God's Spirit will change our nation, transforming the sense that life owes us a living and that being Americans entitles us to all the luxuries we think we deserve. As the New Testament tells us, "Godliness with contentment is great gain" (1 Timothy 6:6). May this contentment, under God, once again become the basis of America's prosperity in spirit and in substance.

Twelve

Commandment Nine:
Tell the Truth

You shall not give false testimony against your neighbor.

—Exodus 20:16

THE LAST FIVE of the Ten Commandments provide a wall of protection around those things we cherish the most. They are there to restrain evil conduct on the one hand and to provide peace of mind and comfort on the other. Jehovah has gone on record for all times saying that He will protect the lives of His people, the marriages of His people, and the property of His people.

In the Ninth Commandment, Jehovah declares that He will protect the reputation and integrity of His people in judicial proceedings that could take away their life or property. His people were to be secure in what to some may be more precious than life itself—their reputation. Proverbs 22:1 says, "A good name is more desirable than great riches," and the Ninth Commandment underscores this fact.

Obviously, the Ninth Commandment applies to lying in general, but its clear thrust is toward those who lie under oath in judicial proceedings or those who seek to destroy reputations by false reports. Such lies are unbelievably serious and can result in judicial forfeiture of property, imprisonment, and even death.

In the early days of our civilization, we did not have available forensic evidence. Fingerprint analysis was not known. Neither blood typing nor DNA evidence was available. There was no hair or fiber analysis, no ballistic testing, and no computer database to check bank records, purchases, travel data, etc. Trials depended on physical evidence such as a body, a weapon, bloody clothes, written documents, and circumstantial evidence.

But more than anything else, trials were and still are determined by the testimony of witnesses. Can you identify the assailant in a lineup? Did you hear an argument? Did you hear a gunshot? Can you describe the thief? Who was in the house when you arrived? How fast was the car traveling? Was there a stop sign at the intersection? Was there ice in front of the store at the time of the accident? What time did it happen?

Answers to questions like these, and thousands more like them, are given by witnesses in thousands of trials and provide the basis for awards of large money damages, or either conviction or acquittal of a crime. The false testimony of a witness can have devastating consequences, which explains the elaborate penalties in our criminal code against perjury and against those who solicit or "suborn" perjury.

Realizing that witnesses are subject to false recall and an imperfect perception of reality, Moses included in the ancient Hebrew law a provision that everything needed to be established by two or more witnesses (Deuteronomy 17:6; 19:15). Yet, even with that safeguard, gross miscarriages of justice could take place.

THE DESTRUCTIVE EFFECTS OF FALSE WITNESSES

After the reign of King Solomon, the kingdom split in two. The northern portion was called Israel, and the southern portion was called Judah. At the time of the prophet Elijah, the king of Israel was Ahab. Ahab's wife, Jezebel, was a scheming, manipulative worshiper of Baal.

According to the biblical record, King Ahab owned a palace and grounds in Samaria, and he longed to possess the vineyard adjoining the palace grounds, which belonged to a man named Naboth. This set up a situation in which four of God's commandments would be violated: coveting, false testimony, murder, and stealing.

Ahab tried to purchase the vineyard from Naboth, but Naboth refused because it was his family's inheritance. Ahab was frustrated. Forgetting his obligation to run a kingdom, his covetousness toward Naboth's vineyard began to consume him so that he went to bed and refused to eat. Finally, the wily Jezebel could take her husband's despondency no more, so she devised a solution.

Letters went out in the king's name to summon the elders of the land to a judicial proceeding. Naboth was placed in their midst. Then Jezebel found "two scoundrels" who accused Naboth of cursing God and the king (1 Kings 21:13). On the testimony of these two false witnesses, Naboth was dragged from the city and stoned to death—no appeal, no lengthy judicial proceeding. Then Jezebel sent word to her husband. "You know the vineyard Naboth wouldn't sell you? Well, you can have it now! He's dead!" (v. 15 NLT).

Of course, Ahab and Jezebel did not get away with this monstrous crime in violation of God's express commandments. They both died violent deaths. Nevertheless, Naboth died because two professional liars bore false witness against him in a judicial proceeding.

The destructive effects of false witnesses are evident in America's court system as well. On January 31, 2000, George H. Ryan, governor of Illinois, suspended all executions in the state because evidence had surfaced that at least twelve death row inmates had been falsely accused by the police. In their desire to show that they were tough on crime, these men who were sworn to uphold the law actually manufactured evidence and suborned false testimony that had the effect of condemning innocent men to their deaths.

I am sure good police officers are revolted by revolving-door justice where those clearly guilty of crime are set free by adroit defense lawyers or lenient judges. However, the police, whose word must be relied on in judicial proceedings, cannot use their power to plant narcotics or weapons on suspects, or to give false testimony under oath during trials.

The *Wall Street Journal* has crusaded in its editorial pages for justice to be done in the case of Gerald Amirault and his mother, Violet Amirault, who ran the Fells Acres day school near Boston, Massachusetts. The Amiraults were caught up in the hysteria that gripped the nation several years ago when all manner of vile, satanic, and sexual rituals were being attributed to day-care centers across the nation. So-called child sexual experts were brought in to question the children. In virtually every instance, the questioner asked leading questions that elicited from the children lurid tales of terrible things. In some cases, the children were terrified and wanted to get back to their parents. However, they were not allowed to unless they either bore witness against their teacher or, in some instances, their own parents. In essence, the little ones didn't know what they were talking about but they were playing back the false testimony that their interrogators had devised. This false testimony resulted in destruction to the business, loss of a sterling reputation, and lengthy prison sentences for both Amiraults.

In a blistering decision, the Massachusetts Governor's Advisory Board overturned the verdict because of demonstrable error. Violet, who is old and in ill health, has been released from prison. Gerald has been released, but the Suffolk County district attorney is determined to try him again.

In recent weeks, television cameras have been focused on the release of prison inmates, most of whom were African American, who were misidentified and falsely accused of rape. Only the advent of DNA testing has provided the clear evidence of innocence to overturn convictions based on "false testimony."

THE NINTH COMMANDMENT AND THE MEDIA

Although the commandments prohibiting having other gods, worshiping idols, dishonoring God's name, violating the Sabbath, committing sexual immorality, or having rapacious greed are seen as offenses to our modern sensibilities, it does seem that the commandment to preserve the integrity of witness testimony in the judicial process is supported by the liberal elites of our nation. The reason is obvious. The liberal temple of worship is the court system. Liberals instinctively oppose anything that compromises their judicial system. Second, the prevailing liberal mind-set is arrayed against restraint of their freedom. Obviously, they would fight any method used by police to imprison the innocent or entrap left-wing radicals, pornographers, or those engaged in social protest movements. However, the Ninth Commandment has a broader meaning beyond judicial proceedings that is indeed an offense to one of the most powerful groups in our nation—the media.

The Ninth Commandment clearly was given to protect reputations from slander. "You shall not give false testimony" about someone's life, character, or activity to destroy that person's reputation. Bernard Goldberg, a former correspondent for CBS News, recently released a book entitled *Bias,* which presents in graphic detail evidence of liberal bias in the media. Falsely labeling a public figure "hard right-wing," "an extremist," or "an intractable obstructionist" when these descriptions do not clearly fit violates the commandment. The smear tactics of the media aimed at judicial appointees is appalling. Worse also is the damage to a business that ambush journalism and hidden cameras can do if the reports are not accurate.

Reporters are often accused of making up slanders intended to destroy the reputation of public figures with whom they disagree. I have been the victim of the false witness of members of the media more times than I like to recall. I have found that reporters often come to a story with a bias that either is theirs personally or is given them by their editors. Then they make up facts to support that bias. One seeming example was in *Newsweek* magazine.

In 1982 CBN was given a television station broadcasting in southern Lebanon on Channel 12. We named it Middle Eastern Television (METV). This station operated under the auspices of Major Haddad, a simple, straightforward Catholic Christian who had been sent to southern Lebanon by then President Camille Chamoun for the purpose of protecting the Christian enclave on the border of Lebanon adjoining northern Israel. Major Haddad was a fighter, but to us he was an honest, hard-working defender of freedom.

After Israel invaded Lebanon, there was a brutal massacre of Palestinian guerrilla fighters and civilians at the Sabra and Shatila refugee camps south of Beirut. No one knew for sure who was responsible, but Israeli general Ariel Sharon has been blamed for allowing the incident to take place. From all of the information given to us, Major Haddad never left southern Lebanon at the time of the massacre and, therefore, had nothing to do with it.

Nevertheless, *Newsweek* created a fictional account, complete with a detailed map, showing how Major Haddad had driven north to Beirut, marched through the Sabra and Shatila camps slaughtering people, and then returned back south. This entire account of Major Haddad's participation seems to be untrue and represented a most flagrant example of a false witness—accusing an innocent man of perpetrating a massacre. By the way, *Newsweek* did not present this story as conjecture but as absolute fact.

I caught *Newsweek* in another egregious lie during the height of the communist insurgency in El Salvador and the reign of the Sandinistas in Nicaragua. I was in San Salvador, the capital of El Salvador, about two weeks before Christmas to do a news report for my television program. I interviewed the president of the country, army leaders, student leaders, former rebel leaders, and citizens. We flew in a Huey helicopter over rebel-held territory and viewed the effects of war. At the end of my visit, I did an on-camera report in front of a small shopping center in the capital city, San Salvador. Behind me was a man in a red Santa Claus suit ringing a bell and shouting, "Feliz Navidad!" I then held up a current copy of *Newsweek* with another of its inaccurate maps. This one showed a rebel stronghold on a hill north of the capital. Our producer flew there by helicopter and walked for hours down the hill. He found not one rebel.

The *Newsweek* article gave false testimony against the government of El Salvador by saying the capital city would fall to the communists by Christmas. I was there two weeks before Christmas, and I suspected *Newsweek* was creating a fabrication to further its left-wing agenda. I showed our television audience the happy Santa Claus, and I showed them the *Newsweek* story. The false witness was palpable and demonstrable. I suppose that *Newsweek* did not expect someone with a television camera crew and Spanish-speaking producer to catch them.

Just a few days before I finished writing this book, Les Moonves, the president of CBS Television, pulled from the lineup a so-called documentary about former President Ronald Reagan that demeaned the reputation of this great president. Reagan was not shown as the strong leader whose powerful resolve accelerated the fall of communism in Eastern Europe. He was not shown as the man whose tax cuts and fiscal policy brought about twenty years of extraordinary prosperity. Instead, he was shown as a bumbling dolt saying something that he had never said in his life: "AIDS was brought on by their sin." While this aged man is suffering from Alzheimer's disease in the twilight of his life, a film producer bears false witness against him, puts words in his mouth that he never spoke, and seeks to destroy his legacy and reputation. A more flagrant violation of the Ninth Commandment would be hard to find.

Imagine the shock of newspaper editors, documentary and

television news producers, and authors if they are told that false witness against the living and the dead is not "artistic expression" or "artistic license" but a violation of God's commandments on a par with murder. To them, this commandment would be an offense.

As I write this, an odd twist on the commandment not to bear false witness is being played out in England. A man named Paul Burrell, who was the butler to Princess Diana, has written a tell-all book about this troubled young lady. Is he telling the truth or is it slander? Of course, for most the issue is whether a domestic employee or any other person enjoying a privileged position should talk about the confidential personal or financial affairs of his employer. But worse than Burrell is the former valet to Prince Charles of England, who has asserted that the prince was involved in an "untoward" incident with a servant. Prince Charles has denied the charge, but the damage to his reputation has been done. If the accusation is false, the valet violated the Ninth Commandment. If the report is true, the valet published slander, which, of necessity, was done either in malice or with a desire to gain financially at the expense of his former employer's reputation.

HOW DOES THE NINTH COMMANDMENT
APPLY TO US?

The average person in America is not a witness in a legal proceeding, does not work in the media, and certainly does not serve royalty. So how does the Ninth Commandment apply to us?

The definition of *slander* is to speak critically of another person with the intent to hurt or defame. In the book of Proverbs, Solomon says that "whoever spreads slander is a fool" (10:18).

In the New Testament, the name given to the chief spiritual enemy of God is "the devil," which means "the accuser." The apostle Paul warns early Christian wives not to be "slanderers" (Titus 2:3). In this verse, the Greek word for "slanderer" is *diabolos*, the same word used for "devil." In other words, those who spread falsehoods against others and who seek to destroy the reputations of others are acting like the devil himself. Those who break the Ninth Commandment are in essence taking on the very nature of the devil, for his task is to slander God, to slander God's people, and to slander all that is holy.

Following are just a few examples of slander that we commonly hear (or say):

"Is it true that Bill got fired for stealing?"

"Is Charlie's business under investigation by the IRS?"

"I have heard that Mary's husband hasn't made his mortgage payments and they are losing their home."

"Is Luke cheating on Priscilla? I heard that he was gay and had a homosexual lover."

"Did you hear that Robert got picked up for possession of narcotics?"

"The business isn't current on its bills. I hear they will soon claim Chapter 11 bankruptcy."

"Did you hear about the guy that stops by Susan's house after her husband has gone to work?"

"Her supervisor says her work is below par. It's only a question of time before they let her go."

If none of these reports are true, they are the product of false witnesses and can kill the reputation of the one to which they refer.

EVEN CHRISTIANS GUILTY OF SLANDER

Recently I was told this story about a man I'll call Jeff, a building contractor. During a time of heated crisis in his marriage, Jeff followed the advice of a counselor and separated from his wife temporarily, giving them both time to cool down. Because his difficult marriage had put a strain on him, his business was suffering.

Then, out of nowhere, someone spread stories that his business was in trouble and his marriage in jeopardy because Jeff was involved in dealing cocaine. In his small community, this kind of story was explosive. Because Jeff was hurting financially and having trouble paying his creditors, people began to believe the rumor was true. New business contracts dried up. Suppliers and banks with whom he had worked for years had their suspicions aroused as well.

Jeff was forced into bankruptcy. In a desperate attempt to save his reputation and livelihood, he sold his home to pay off debts, and this additional strain pushed his wife to file for divorce. Whereas he had hoped to pull his marriage and his life back together, he saw it all fall into ruins. Then came another crippling blow.

Jeff eventually traced the rumors about himself to their source: a man who occasionally attended his church and who was also in land development—in effect, a business competitor. That this man had spread false testimony about him was bad enough, but the lies had been picked up and repeated enough by other believers in his own church that they slowly spread throughout the community. Fellow Christians, under the subtle rubric of "praying for Jeff" and "expressing concern" for him, eroded his reputation and ultimately shook the foundations of his life. Jeff is on the way to rebuilding his reputation and his business. But after learning that Christians helped assassinate his character, it is no wonder that he now says, "I have a hard time wanting anything to do with Christians. It's going to take a long time for me to trust them again."

This type of vicious undercutting of people's reputations occurs all over America. It has been rightly said that great minds talk about ideas, but small minds talk about people. Petty gossips are offended if told they are sinning, but they are.

TRUTH IN OUR HEARTS

The Bible says that no "unwholesome talk [should] come out of [our] mouths, but only what is helpful for building others up according to their needs, that it may benefit those who listen" (Ephesians 4:29). It is the intention of Jehovah that we should be zealous to protect our neighbor's reputations and we will only speak the truth in love (Ephesians 4:13). In turn, it is His desire that we are each safe from those vicious lies that tear down our reputations, our families, and our life's work.

Unless we embrace the idea that there is a God whose words are true and absolute, unless we accept the challenge to be truthful in all our ways, we are a society of people living in our twilight hours. No nation, no human being, can stand for long on a foundation of untruth and lies.

In 1997 I was the controlling shareholder of a large and quite successful media company, the stock of which was traded on the New York Stock Exchange. Two things seemed obvious to us. On the one hand, the prices we had to pay Hollywood film producers for programs had reached such a level that a cable rerun of a popular show was selling at a price of $1 million for each episode. Multiplied by 120 episodes, the commitment for just one program, which might not prove successful, would have been $120 million. On the other hand, stock prices seemed quite high, and might not stay that high forever. So we put the company up for sale and were fortunate to find two highly motivated buyers—the Walt Disney Company and Rupert Murdoch's News Corporation. The sums we were discussing began with a "b," not an "m," yet at a crucial point in the discussion Rupert Murdoch said, "On this I give you my word." Nothing more. No lengthy contract. Just his word. But to me that meant more than the tightest contract our New York lawyers could draft. This man is enormously successful financially, and this simple statement may go a long way to explaining his success. In business, people put great stock in dealing with people whose word is their bond.

For all told, it's truth—and the virtue of truthfulness—that paves our public dealings as well as our private relationships with stability. And it is God's Word alone that admonishes us to tell the simple truth when a lie would be easier, and to live by eternal truth instead.

I believe it is time for us to return again, as a nation and as individuals, to a commitment to truth. May God plant this desire in our hearts—that we may become a people who are eager to turn away from lying words and obey the words of Jesus when He said, "Let your yes be yes, and your no be no."

THIRTEEN

Commandment Ten:
Be Content with What You Have

You shall not covet . . . anything that belongs to your neighbor.

—EXODUS 20:17

IN 1989 Saddam Hussein, the dictator of Iraq, looked across the sand to the small, defenseless nation of Kuwait. He was fascinated by what he saw: billions of barrels of easily accessible oil, a portfolio of overseas investments valued in the hundreds of billions of dollars, and people wallowing in the lap of luxury. Hussein had a powerful army; Kuwait had virtually none. In a matter of hours, his forces could roll into Kuwait, and that treasure trove of wealth would be his.

What went through the mind of Saddam Hussein is called coveting. To "covet" is to desire ardently, to set the mind on, to wish for more. Coveting is not in itself sinful. In the New Testament, the apostle Paul instructs the church at Corinth to "covet earnestly the best gifts" (1 Corinthians 12:31 KJV). Christians are to covet the attributes of God. The reason that it is appropriate to covet after God and His righteousness is simple—God is infinite; therefore, there is enough of God for everyone. God is never diminished, so your receipt of the fullness of God's spiritual blessings in no way takes from me, nor does my receipt of God's nature take from you.

There is nothing wrong with coveting what is in unlimited supply, any more than it is sinful to earnestly desire to breathe fresh air or bask in the rays of the sun.

The Tenth Commandment does not forbid all coveting, only coveting what is in short supply and belongs to someone else—his spouse, his house, his employees, his automobile, his success, his job, or his possessions.

The first Iraq war began because of coveting—first the thought, then the deed. The armed forces of Iraq invaded Kuwait and quickly took over. Hopeless Kuwaitis saw their lives destroyed, their women raped, and their men killed or imprisoned and tortured. The little country, despite its great wealth, lay helpless before the armed might of its neighbor.

Of course, had Saddam's mind not been blinded by covetousness, he would have realized that the nations of the world were not about to permit a megalomaniac to gain hegemony over the key source of the world's oil. Soon a great force was assembled that drove the Iraqis from Kuwait, crushed their military, and imposed punitive sanctions on the nation. Saddam's refusal to abide by the United Nation's mandates led to Gulf War II, the downfall of his regime, the death of his sons, and the occupation of his country by the armed forces of the United States and its Coalition partners.

All because Saddam violated the Tenth Commandment.

THE CONSEQUENCES OF COVETING

In the 1930s another dictator named Adolf Hitler began to covet what belonged to his neighbors. He wanted the Sudetenland in Czechoslovakia. He wanted the Rhineland. He wanted the port of Danzig in Poland. Ultimately, he coveted all of Europe and Russia. The excuse he used was fraudulent. He wasn't a coveting aggressor; he merely needed *lebensraum,* or "living space," for Germany.

His coveting caused the march of jack-booted troops and tank-led panzer divisions to destroy the heartland of Europe. Nazi dive-bombers ruthlessly destroyed cities and villages. Homes and factories were demolished. The roads were choked with a flood of displaced refugees. The air was filled with the sobs and moans of helpless people. Before the madness ended, fifty million human beings had been slaughtered.

All because one madman coveted what belonged to his neighbors.

As I review the broad panorama of civilization, it is difficult to find any of the empire builders of history—Alexander the Great, the Romans, Attila the Hun, the Goths and Visigoths, the Vikings, the Mohammedans, Genghis Khan and the Mongols, the Ottoman Turks, the Spanish empire, Napoleon, the colonial powers—who were not first motivated by coveting what was not theirs. They wanted wealth, plunder, unbridled sexuality with captured women, domination over others, power, glory, and fame. Only God Himself knows the suffering that the violation of the Tenth Commandment has visited on the people of planet earth since its beginning. But God clearly knows what it is in the soul of some men who lust until they have accumulated unto themselves empires, kingdoms, and vast wealth.

In the 1920s John D. Rockefeller was the world's richest man. He was once asked, "How much wealth is enough?" Rockefeller replied, "Just a little bit more!"

People can either earn fame and fortune in a legitimate fashion, or they can scheme up ways to take it away from someone else. They can be content with having food, clothing, shelter, and a loving family, or they can violate the commandment, "You shall not covet . . . anything that belongs to your neighbor."

THE COVETOUSNESS OF A KING

Consider the case of David, who was called "a man after [God's] own heart" (1 Samuel 13:14). David was the king of Israel, and he was permitted to keep a harem of women. He was first married to the daughter of King Saul, his predecessor. Then he married Abigail, the widow of a churlish rich man named Nabal. Then to please his fancy, he took other women and had children with them. When Saul died and David was crowned king, David took Saul's wives and concubines for himself. To put it mildly, this vigorous king was hardly sex-starved and lonely.

Yet one spring day—"at the time when kings go off to war" (2 Samuel 11:1)—David stayed home with nothing much to do. As he walked on the roof of his palace, he noticed a beautiful woman taking a bath on a nearby rooftop. This woman was another man's wife, and David began to covet her. Coveting is the wellspring of action. As king, David could have whatever he wanted. This woman was so attractive that David had his servants bring her to him, and he had sex with her. First coveting, then adultery.

But the story doesn't end there. After a few months, the woman sent word to David that she was pregnant. So David began damage control. Her husband was in the field with the army, so David had him brought home. David entertained him in the palace, got him drunk, and sent him home to sleep with his wife. Unfortunately, this man was so righteous that he refused to enjoy the comforts of his wife and his home while his fellow comrades were out on the battlefield. So, in a desperate attempt to cover up his adultery, David arranged for the husband to be killed in battle. Then he took the woman, Bathsheba, as his wife.

By now David had broken three of the commandments of Jehovah. First, he coveted another man's wife. Then he committed adultery. Then he committed murder. God sent a prophet to David who said, in effect, "What have you done? How unbelievably selfish of you. God gave you everything and, if that wasn't enough, He would have given you much more. Why did you do this thing? Now the sword will never depart from your house." Although David repented of his sin and was forgiven by God, his children suffered the tragic consequences of his covetousness.

EVERYDAY EXAMPLES OF COVETING

Consider this somewhat typical fictional account. A man works in an office. He is a strong churchgoer. His wife is attractive, intelligent, a good mother, and a great life partner. But in the office, working closely by him, is a married twenty-something hard body with a saucy smile, clear complexion, and silky hair. Sitting across from her day after day, Mr. Typical Office Worker begins to fantasize that someday she might be his. He desires her; he covets her for himself. Already he has violated the Tenth Commandment. But is that all?

The chances are, Mr. Typical Office Worker is fooling himself. But if not, will adultery result? A breakup of his wonderful home? Even the murder of the young lady's husband? This is not just the stuff of fiction—it can and does happen in real life.

Or consider this. Two salesmen work for the same company. One is barely making his quota; the other is wildly successful. Salesman A could ask himself what he could learn from the success of his associate, Salesman B. What techniques could he employ? Is the secret to Salesman B's success that he works harder or has a more positive attitude? Salesman A could even go to his associate and humbly ask for help so that his performance could improve.

Or he could grow jealous and begin to covet Salesman B's success. He could try to steal B's customers or seek to get part of his territory. He could begin to spread falsehoods about Salesman B that could result in the loss of B's job.

Violating the Tenth Commandment easily leads to stealing and slander. Regrettably, what is called cutthroat competition to steal markets, concepts, customers, and reputations is not only perfectly legal, it is often commended by those who prize material success above all else.

COVETING GUARANTEES FAILURE

The Bible tells us of a time in the history of mankind when people wanted to build a monument to their achievement that would reach up to heaven. They were building a one-world government intended as a center of rebellion against Almighty God. According to the Bible, God came down to see the tower, then He scattered the people so they would be unable to unite in rebellion. God's reaction to this human activity is most instructive. "This people," He said, "have one mind and they speak with one voice. Now nothing that they propose to do will be impossible to them" (see Genesis 11:1–9 author's paraphrase).

When every member of a team is working for the good of the team, the team will win. When all the members of a company are working together, they will succeed. Nothing will be impossible for them.

A few years ago, a man named Napoleon Hill popularized a book called *Think and Grow Rich*. Hill's book contained heavy New Age overtones, as well as some biblical concepts—one of which was the creation of what he called a "Master Plan Alliance." His thought is sound. To achieve success, assemble three or four people who agree wholeheartedly on the plan. There is to be no dispute, no backbiting, no rancor—just total agreement among the members of the Master Plan Alliance.

Compare this concept of success based on unity with the actions of an organization whose members are intensely jealous of each other's success, who covet each other's possessions, who lust after each other's spouses, and who spare no effort to diminish the respect and achievements of other members of the team. This is an organization where the prevailing ethic is "cover your backside." Harmony guarantees success; coveting and division guarantee failure. In the words of Jesus, "Every city or household divided against itself will not stand" (Matthew 12:25). And consider the incredibly bitter feuds that develop among brothers and sisters who covet the share of their parents' estate that was given to another sibling.

OUR FASCINATION WITH COVETING

Our nation is given over to that which will cause coveting. *Forbes* magazine publishes a list each year of the 400 richest people in America. This article causes people to desire to possess the wealth of Bill Gates, Warren Buffett, Michael Dell, Larry Ellison, the Walton family, the Mars family, and so on. Several years ago, a television show called *Lives of the Rich and Famous* was calculated, without question, to stir up coveting for mansions, yachts, imported sports cars, designer clothes, priceless paintings, and life on the French Riviera or in the Hamptons.

On a less opulent scale, virtually all television advertising is calculated to stir up lust for things or for a different lifestyle or for sensuous-looking women. Coveting and lust go hand in hand. Each contains the seed of actions that cause overt violation of God's laws and the laws of the land. Coveting precedes shoplifting, grand theft auto, and armed robbery; coveting precedes adultery and rape; coveting precedes breaking and entering and murder; and coveting can lead to perjury under oath in a court of law. Coveting can lead to trafficking in narcotics, counterfeiting, money laundering, and white-collar crime, or it can lead to identity theft and fraudulent use of credit cards. Coveting can even lead to blood feuds and wars.

The Sixth, Seventh, Eighth, and Ninth Commandments all require overt actions. It is possible for a devout person to say, in the words of a rich young ruler who came to ask Jesus for advice, "All these I have kept since I was a boy" (Mark 10:20). After all, we haven't murdered anyone, we haven't committed armed robbery, we haven't carried out an adulterous affair, and we haven't lied as a witness in court.

In many ways we are like the apostle Paul, who had maintained all of the outward evidence of piety. But then the Tenth Commandment, which deals with an attitude of the mind and spirit, reached out and seized him. Here are his words:

> I would never have known that coveting is wrong if the law had not said, "Do not covet." But sin took advantage of this law and aroused all kinds of forbidden desires within me! . . . I felt fine when I did not understand what the law demanded. But when I learned the truth, I realized I had broken the law and was a sinner, doomed to die. . . . I love God's law with all my heart. But there is another law at work within me that is at war with my mind. . . . Who will free me from this life that is dominated by sin? Thank God! The answer is in Jesus Christ our Lord. (Romans 7:7–9, 22–25 NLT)

The apostle Paul realized that the inner urges of his being that pushed toward self-gratification could only be curbed by a spiritual transformation in Jesus Christ—what is termed being "born again" (John 3:3). As he put it, "If anyone is in Christ, he is a new creation; the old has gone, the new has come!" (2 Corinthians 5:17).

To Paul, the law of God was something holy and good for our benefit on earth. But to him, the greatest blessing of the commandments of God was that they served as a tutor to lead us to Christ (Galatians 3:24). Christ, he said, is the end of the law for believers (Romans 10:4). The law is a shadow of good things to come, but the ultimate reality is a heavenly existence with Jesus Christ (Hebrews 10:1).

Of course, to today's liberal thinkers God's commands are a foolish restriction on the actualization of human potential—an offense through and through.

In the final analysis, it is self-will—the will apart from God—that essentially makes us rebels.

BREAKING THE SPELL OF SELF

Today, as America lies under the influence of those who promote radical individualism and feed our self-will, we as a nation are becoming numb to the voices of God and conscience. We have fallen under the spell of the self.

James Hillman, a leader in the field of depth psychology, wrote *The Force of Character and the Lasting Life,* an exploration of what Hillman believes constitutes "character." In it, Hillman praises "self" because, in his view, self is "without limiting characteristics. Self conflates with God."

In other words, the self is God. Every one of us is our own deity. This is the idea that is taking hold in America today. From its liberal proponents on down, this idea has wormed its way throughout our culture—into government, education, law, finance, science, and our social welfare agencies. Anyone who opposes the supremacy of self and the self-will apart from God is an enemy.

Hillman is, of course, just one voice among the pantheon of liberal thinkers who promote the radical individualism that drives America today. There are many others, each one promoting the idea that to free the human spirit from all limitations is to save humanity and reform American society. With unlimited freedom, man will rise to unprecedented spiritual heights. Such thinking is idealistic at best. At worst, it is daily undermining the Judeo-Christian foundation of our society.

One of the spiritual giants of the last century, A. W. Tozer, foresaw the dangers inherent in promoting a spirituality that places man at the center of all things and proclaims the self as supreme. The truth is, when we are given over to our self-centered desires and living apart from God, we become corrupt beings. Created by God and pronounced "good" in his eyes, every one of us has pursued our own will, which has led us to harm other people. After breaking the First Commandment, we are bound to break those that come after. We have all sinned against both God and man. We are sinners, and the evil intentions that worm their way out of us numb our consciences and slowly lull our souls to sleep. If we are not awakened, we will experience the sleep of spiritual death. This is the end that lies ahead if we spend our whole lives apart from God, defying His laws and worshiping in the cult of self.

Terrible as it is to be spiritually lost, this is not a state in which we are stranded without hope. Tozer wrote, "In the Bible, the offer of pardon on the part of God is conditioned upon intention to reform on the part of man."

Once we awaken to the fact that we have ignored God and broken His laws, we can turn back to God and receive grace. Repenting is not so much a matter of feeling bad about what we've done or neglected to do. We may indeed feel sorry for violating God's laws when we recognize the damage we have done to others and to the condition of our own souls. Sometimes emotions get in the way of true conversion and ongoing spiritual growth. The churches in America are full of people who feel bad about wrongdoing. And while that's a beginning, true mature conversion of spirit, the kind that alters behavior, is a matter of starting over with right convictions—as Tozer put it, with full "intention" in our hearts to "reform."

BECOMING SPIRITUALLY REFORMED

What does it mean to spiritually reform? Who will reform us?

The Bible tells us that we are saved from the penalty of our sins if we trust in the sacrifice of Jesus Christ, who shed his blood on the cross to save us. "To all who [receive] Him" into their hearts by faith, says the apostle John, "to those who [believe] in His name," God gives "the right to become children of God—children born not of natural descent . . . but born of God" (John 1:12–13). Those who ask God for this great gift of salvation receive it, and none are turned away. This is how we are born into the family of God.

To receive Jesus Christ into our hearts is to encounter his Holy Spirit. It is this Spirit that moves into the deepest places inside us, down into our souls, and begins to bring to light the "intentions" of our hearts (Romans 8:27; 1 Corinthians 2:10). It is this ongoing operation, the discerning work of the Holy Spirit, that daily shows us how to distinguish between the selfish intentions of our natural humanity and the purer intentions of the new force in our soul— the Spirit of Christ (Hebrews 4:12). As we leave behind our self-centered attitudes, we are reformed from within as the Spirit of God gives us new courage and strength, urging us to be self-giving and to act in kindness, goodness, gentleness, peacefulness . . . and love (Galatians 5:22).

To be reformed in spirit is not to become legalists who point their fingers at others and judge their wrongdoing. It is to have the character of Christ formed within us (Galatians 4:19). In this way, we emerge into the world as new creations (2 Corinthians 5:17), the obedient sons and daughters of the living God. In this way, by an inner and daily reliance upon God's Spirit and grace, He helps us to mature in spirit and obey His law more and more perfectly.

God willingly gives us His Spirit if we humble ourselves and ask. By His Spirit He will reform us from within, creating a new people who are free from the law of sin and death . . . free to obey the laws of God, which give life. He will make us ready for the work that needs to be done in our nation at this crucial hour.

What Our Nation Needs

If we look at the evidence—the murder of the unborn, the rampant violence, the adultery, stealing, and lying that characterizes America—we know that we need a sweeping spiritual revival at this hour in our nation's history. We do not need conversions of sentiment that give us nice, warm feelings about God and other people. We need a transformation of character brought about by the work of the Holy Spirit. We need this as individuals. And if we are to survive as a "nation under God," we desperately need this as a country.

Throughout this book we have looked closely at our need to regain respect for God's law. It is true that, as a people, Americans react indignantly when liberal groups try to remove a stone tablet inscribed with the Ten Commandments from an Alabama courthouse. We bristle when someone suggests we change the Pledge of Allegiance by cutting out the words "under God." We march in protest of laws promoting abortion and lobby our legislators when bills come before Congress that support alternative lifestyles that defy God's Word. The dismantling of Christian morality on which America is founded must end. Our protests and public work are indeed outward signs of our devotion to God—necessary, even critical, in a world where voices and votes still sway the opinions of our lawmakers.

But we must also remember that in God's economy, to love Him is to obey Him. We obey and demonstrate our love for God both in acts of worship and private devotion *and* in the way we act toward others in our everyday world—our coworkers, fellow students, and neighbors. For as Jesus said, "'Love the LORD your God with all your heart and with all your soul and with all your mind.' This is the first and greatest commandment. And the second is like it: 'Love your neighbor as yourself'" (Matthew 22:39).

The kind of conversion we need—every single man, woman, and child in America—is the kind that makes us living witnesses to the reality and presence of a holy and loving God. We are to stand for both of these life-affirming characteristics in our streets, schools, offices, as well as in our polling places and public meetings. For as the late Christian apologist Francis Schaeffer once observed, love that is rooted in righteousness is still "the mark of the Christian."

EPILOGUE

An Action Plan

THE ESTEEMED BRITISH STATESMAN William Wilberforce, whose determined decades-long assault on the British slave trade led to its final abolition in Great Britain and the United States, wrote:

> It is a truth attested by the history of all ages and countries, and established on the authority of the ablest writers, both ancient and modern . . . that the religion and morality of a country, especially of every free community, are inseparably connected with its preservation and welfare; that their flourishing or declining state is the sure indication of its tending to prosperity or decay. It has even been expressly laid down, that a people grossly corrupt are incapable of liberty.

Wilberforce was right, as were the countless statesmen who made it crystal-clear that no free nation can endure without public morality—and, in turn, there can be no public morality, to quote George Washington, "in exclusion of religious principle."

No nation in history has survived that legitimized sodomy and gross sexual excess. No nation in history has survived whose leaders plundered future generations to ensure their continuance in power. No nation can survive that refuses to pass on its history, traditions, and moral standards to its youth. No nation can survive that cannibalizes its unborn for its own convenience.

Has America gone too far, or can we as a nation come back from the abyss that is yawning before us?

Here are the facts. According to the CBS television program *60 Minutes,* Americans spend as much money on adult entertainment as they do on professional sports attendance. Vile smut peddlers are now mainstream, and hard-core pornography has become a significant profit center for major American corporations. What does this do to family stability and child rearing?

One Christian denomination in America has not only welcomed sodomites, it has ordained as a bishop a man who left his wife and has been engaging in a homosexual relationship with another man for almost fifteen years. Recently, the United States Supreme Court has ruled not only that homosexuality is permitted in America, but it is now an activity *guaranteed by the United States Constitution.*

Since 1973, when the Supreme Court declared the killing of unborn babies was a "constitutional right," Americans have slaughtered as many as forty-five million unborn lives.

While a flood of evil has been assaulting our land, the Supreme Court and lesser federal courts, joined by the educational establishment, have been unremitting in their efforts to strip America of the moral and spiritual influences we must have to cure the moral rot eating away our nation's heart.

A November 2003 survey commissioned by a group known as the Foundation for Individual Rights in Education (FIRE) revealed a shocking ignorance among college students and school administrators of our most fundamental constitutional rights. The survey conducted by the Center for Survey Research and Analysis at the University of Connecticut revealed that one out of every four undergraduates could not mention any freedoms guaranteed by the

First Amendment; only a 30 percent minority felt that freedom of religion is a constitutionally protected right. Only 6 percent of college and university administrators and 2 percent of students named freedom of religion as the freedom that the First Amendment addresses before all others.

Only 36 percent of administrators in private institutions and 50 percent at public institutions believed that religious individuals should be free to spread their beliefs "by whatever lawful means they choose." Twenty-four percent believe they have the legal right to prohibit a student religious group from trying to convert the students to its religion, yet an amazing 49 percent of administrators at private schools reported *mandatory* noncurriculum programs, "the goal of which is to lead [students] *to value all sexual preferences and to recognize the relativity of these values compared to the values of their upbringing*" (emphasis added).

Isn't this appalling? Few administrators recognize religious freedom, a sizable portion believe that religious freedom can be arbitrarily restricted, and almost half believe that mandatory homosexual brainwashing of college and university students is warranted. This is how far our society has moved from the principles of its founding.

But there is more. The federal deficit in this fiscal year is forecast at $500 billion. Our annual trade deficit is comparable to that amount. The United States is far and away the world's largest debtor, financing its profligate ways with foreign borrowing estimated at *one billion dollars every day!* Our total national indebtedness, including Social Security and Medicare, is estimated at $34 trillion.

If the hand of Almighty God turns against us, there are already set in place elements that could bring about a financial debacle of unimagined proportions—a debacle that could serve to humble each one of us as it rips away our employment, our savings, our homes, our lifestyles, and our power as a nation.

If the past is any guide, we know that a righteous God will not hold back His judgment forever. A great nation can slowly be destroyed by pervasive moral decay. We sow the seeds of our own destruction, or God Himself can strike sudden devastating blows—violent earthquakes, hurricanes and tornadoes, massive flooding, extended drought, widespread disease, even the impact of an asteroid. Or God can raise up fierce enemies who delight only in destruction and death.

Knowingly or unknowingly, the ACLU, the National Abortion Rights Action League, Planned Parenthood, the National Organization of Women, the Gay-Lesbian Alliance, the American Atheists, Marxists, People for the American Way, Americans United for Separation of Church and State, advocates of political correctness in education, and all of their allies across the land in Congress, the state legislatures, and the media are hastening the destruction of the United States of America and the freedoms and lifestyle we all enjoy.

If any normal homeowner found a group of people armed with jackhammers hacking away the foundations of his beloved home, the chances are he would do whatever was in his power to stop them. Yet for one hundred years the enemies of our national homeland have been pounding away at the moral and spiritual pillars that support our house. They speak of their desire to be free from religion, free from religious restraint, and free to "do their thing," regardless of its effect on the rest of us.

When we cry out in horror that they must be stopped or our house will be destroyed, five nonelected men and women in black robes often vote together and issue decrees that on the one hand make undermining our moral foundation a constitutional right, while on the other hand forbid our representatives from stopping it.

So what must we do while there is still time?

WHAT YOU CAN DO

• First, we must appeal to the One whom the patriarch Abraham called "the Judge of all the earth" (Genesis 18:25). He is higher than any government of man, any congress of man, any president of man, and certainly higher than any court of man.

Our nation is in danger, and it behooves us as a people to humble ourselves and cry out to God to stop the United States Supreme Court from unjustly usurping power. Our God is a God of power and justice. If the hearts of His people are humbly turned to Him from evil ways, He promises to hear our prayers and heal our land (2 Chronicles 7:14).

We need to have a sense of urgency. I am not talking about performing one more meaningless religious exercise, but praying the desperate prayer of one whose very life is in jeopardy. A prayer like that of John Knox, who cried out, "Lord, give me Scotland or I die!"

• Secondly, it is essential that moral reformation begin with each of us. It is hardly adequate for us to attend rallies protesting the removal of the Ten Commandments from public buildings if we are breaking the commandments in our private lives. We need to exalt Jehovah God to the preeminent place in our lives and tear down the idols that we so easily erect in our hearts.

Does our speech exalt the Lord, and do we set His day apart? Do we honor our mother and father? Do we respect the human dignity of our fellow man? Are we honest in our dealings with others? Are we sexually pure and faithful to our spouse in thought and deed? Do we refrain from slandering others, and is our word our bond? Do we resist coveting what someone else possesses?

If we live the commandments of God, then our lives will prove a far more effective testimony than any stone tablet, no matter where it is situated.

• Third, we must sound a note of outrage at the actions of the federal courts. We must show our fellow citizens and our elected officials the utter absurdity of a nation of 270 million free men and women surrendering control of the most vital aspects of our national life to five nonelected judges.

— We must protest and publish. We must demonstrate the truth of our position from the historic record. We must organize effective symposia, town meetings, marches, or rallies. We must write papers for learned journals and insist on their publication.

— We should consider taking part in radio and television call-in programs, teaching a Sunday school class to educate our fellow parishioners about the crisis, putting up lawn signs, distributing bumper stickers, and writing letters to the editor of our local newspaper.

— We must familiarize ourselves with the issues, support the passage of judiciary-limiting legislation, contact our local officials to encourage them to support religious freedom, and, of course, register to vote.

— Then we must put together powerful grass-roots lobbying efforts to show members of the United States Senate that we will not tolerate a few left-wing special interest groups making puppets of individual senators in judicial confirmation proceedings. We must demand that the rules of the United States Senate be changed to forbid a minority of forty senators from seizing control of the judicial confirmation process and frustrating the clear judicial advice and consent mechanism specified in the United States Constitution. We must insist that senators who wish to hijack majority rule in judicial confirmations pay a heavy price, both in subsequent primaries and the general elections.

Our work must be determined and steadfast. Despite temporary setbacks, we must never stop pushing forward until judicial tyranny is defeated and the Constitution is once again given its central place in our government.

• Finally, if all else fails, our efforts may establish sufficient moral outrage in our nation that the Congress and state legislatures will once again take back the power given them under the Constitution. The United States Congress was in no way intended to be subservient to the Supreme Court. In fact, the reverse is true. Congress abdicated its power, and over the years the Court seized that power. But just because a thief steals something not his and keeps it without protest is no reason that the rightful owner cannot reclaim what is his. Congress can reclaim its power if the moral and political will exists for it to do so.

Remember, the Supreme Court has no enforcement power other than what is given it by the legislature and the chief executive. As Thomas Jefferson is said to have remarked, "Marshall has made his decree; now let him enforce it." Civil disobedience is odious, but not when there is disobedience to unlawful and unconstitutional decrees. Let us hope such a confrontation will not be necessary. Let us hope America regains its lost spiritual heritage.

Let us fervently hope and pray that, in truth, it may once more truly be said that America is "one nation under God."

APPENDIX

ALABAMA (1901)

Preamble: "We, the people of the State of Alabama, in order to establish justice, insure domestic tranquility, and secure the blessings of liberty to ourselves and our posterity, *invoking the favor and guidance of Almighty God,*[1] do ordain and establish the following Constitution and form of government for the State of Alabama."

ALASKA (R. 1956 O. 1959)

"We the people of Alaska, *grateful to God* and to those who founded our nation and pioneered this great land, in order to secure and transmit to succeeding generations our heritage of political, civil, and religious liberty within the Union of States, do ordain and establish this constitution for the State of Alaska."

ARIZONA (1910)

Preamble: "We the people of the State of Arizona, *grateful to Almighty God for our liberties,* do ordain this Constitution."

ARKANSAS (1874)

Preamble: "We, the people of the State of Arkansas, *grateful to Almighty God for the privilege of choosing our own form of government, for our civil and religious liberty, and desiring to perpetuate its blessings and secure the same to our selves and posterity,* do ordain and establish this Constitution."

CALIFORNIA

Preamble: "We, the People of the State of California, *grateful to Almighty God for our freedom, in order to secure and perpetuate its blessings,* do establish this Constitution."

COLORADO (1876)

Preamble: "We, the people of Colorado, *with profound reverence for the Supreme Ruler of the Universe* ... do ordain and establish this constitution for the State of Colorado."

CONNECTICUT (1965)

Preamble: "The People of Connecticut acknowledging with gratitude, the good providence of God, in having permitted them to enjoy a free government; do ... hereby, after a careful consideration and revision, ordain and establish the following constitution and form of civil government."

DELAWARE (1897)

Preamble: *"Through Divine goodness, all men have by nature the rights of worshiping and serving their Creator according to the dictates of their consciences, ..."*

ARTICLE I.§1. Freedom of religion.

Section 1. *Although it is the duty of all men frequently to assemble together for the public worship of Almighty God; and piety and morality, on which the prosperity of communities depends, are hereby promoted ..."*

FLORIDA (1885/1968)

Preamble: "We, the people of the State of Florida, *being grateful to Almighty God for our constitutional liberty,* in order to secure its benefits, perfect our government, insure domestic tranquility, maintain public order, and guarantee equal civil and political rights to all, do ordain and establish this constitution."

GEORGIA (1777/1983)

Preamble: "To perpetuate the principles of free government, insure justice to all, preserve peace, promote the interest and happiness of the citizen and of the family, and transmit to posterity the enjoyment of liberty, *we the people of Georgia, relying upon the protection and guidance of Almighty God,* do ordain and establish this Constitution."

ARTICLE I. SECTION 1. RIGHTS OF PERSONS

Paragraph III. Freedom of conscience.

Each person has the natural and inalienable right to worship God, each according to the dictates of the person's own conscience; and no human authority should, in any case, control or interfere with such rights of conscience.

HAWAII

Preamble: "We, the people of Hawaii, *grateful for Divine Guidance,* and mindful of our Hawaiian heritage and uniqueness as an island State, ... do hereby ordain and establish this constitution for the State of Hawaii."

IDAHO (1890)

Preamble: "We, the people of the state of Idaho, *grateful to Almighty God for our freedom,* to secure its blessings and promote our common welfare do establish this Constitution."

ARTICLE 1. SECTION 4. GUARANTY OF RELIGIOUS LIBERTY.

"The exercise and enjoyment of religious faith and worship shall forever be guaranteed; and no person shall be denied any civil or political right, privilege, or capacity on account of his religious opinions."

ILLINOIS (1970)

Preamble: "We, the People of the State of Illinois—*grateful to Almighty God for the civil, political and religious liberty which He has permitted us to enjoy and seeking His blessing upon our endeavors*... do ordain and establish this Constitution for the State of Illinois."

INDIANA (1851/2001)

Preamble: "To the end, that justice be established, public order maintained, and liberty perpetuated; WE, the People of the State of Indiana, *grateful to ALMIGHTY GOD for the free exercise of the right to choose our own form of government,* do ordain this Constitution."

ARTICLE 1. S1. : "We declare, *That all people are created equal; that they are endowed by their CREATOR with certain inalienable rights."*

ARTICLE 1. SECTION 2. RIGHT TO WORSHIP

"All people shall be secured in the natural right to worship ALMIGHTY GOD, according to the dictates of their own consciences."

IOWA

Preamble: "We the people of the state of Iowa, *grateful to the Supreme Being for the blessings hitherto enjoyed, and feeling our dependence on Him for a continuation of those blessings,* do ordain and establish a free and independent government, by the name of the State of Iowa ... "

KANSAS

Preamble: "We, the people of Kansas, *grateful to Almighty God for our civil and religious privileges,* in order to insure the full enjoyment of our rights as American citizens, do ordain and establish this constitution of the state of Kansas."

Religious liberty. *"The right to worship God according to the dictates of conscience shall never be infringed."*

KENTUCKY (1792/1891)

Preamble: "We, the people of the Commonwealth of Kentucky, *grateful to Almighty God for the civil, political and religious liberties we enjoy, and invoking the continuance of these blessings,* do ordain and establish this Constitution."

Section 1: "All men are, by nature, free and equal, and have certain inherent and inalienable rights, among which may be reckoned . . . Second: *The right of worshipping Almighty God according to the dictates of their consciences."*

LOUISIANA (1974)

Preamble: "We, the people of Louisiana, *grateful to Almighty God for the civil, political, economic, and religious liberties we enjoy* . . . do ordain and establish this constitution."

MAINE

Preamble: "We the people of Maine, . . . *acknowledging with grateful hearts the goodness of the Sovereign Ruler of the Universe in affording us an opportunity, so favorable to the design; and, imploring God's aid and direction in its accomplishment,* do agree to form ourselves into a free and independent State, by the style and title of the State of Maine and do ordain and establish the following Constitution for the government of the same."

Section 3. *"All individuals have a natural and unalienable right to worship Almighty God according to the dictates of their own consciences, and no person shall be hurt, molested or restrained in that person's liberty or estate for worshipping God in the manner and season most agreeable to the dictates of that person's own conscience."*

MARYLAND (1867/2002)

Preamble: "We, the People of the State of Maryland, *grateful to Almighty God for our civil and religious liberty,* and taking into our serious consideration the best means of establishing a good Constitution in this State for the sure foundation and more permanent security thereof, declare . . ."

Art. 36 *"That as it is the duty of every man to worship God in such a manner as he thinks most acceptable to Him . . ."*

Art. 37 *"That no religious test ought ever to be required as a qualification for any office of profit or trust in this State, other than a declaration of the belief in the existence of God;"*

Art. 39 "That the manner of administering an oath or affirmation to any person, ought to be such as those of the religious persuasion, profession, or denomination, of which he is a member, *generally esteem the most effectual confirmation by the attestation of the Divine Being."*

MASSACHUSETTS
Preamble: ". . . We, therefore, the people of Massachusetts, *acknowledging, with grateful hearts, the goodness of the great Legislator of the universe, in affording us, in the course of His providence,* an opportunity, deliberately and peaceably, without fraud, violence or surprise, of entering into an original, explicit, and solemn compact with each other; and of forming a new constitution of civil government, for ourselves and posterity; and devoutly imploring His direction in so interesting a design, do agree upon, ordain and establish the following Declaration of Rights, and Frame of Government, as the Constitution of the Commonwealth of Massachusetts."

Article II. "It is the right as well as the duty of all men in society, publicly, and at stated seasons to *worship the Supreme Being, the great Creator and Preserver of the universe. And no subject shall be hurt, molested, or restrained, in his person, liberty, or estate, for worshipping God in the manner and season most agreeable to the dictates of his own conscience;* or for his religious profession or sentiments; provided he doth not disturb the public peace, or obstruct others in their religious worship."

MICHIGAN
Preamble: "We, the people of the State of Michigan, *grateful to Almighty God for the blessings of freedom,* and earnestly desiring to secure these blessings undiminished to ourselves and our posterity, do ordain and establish this constitution."

ARTICLE I, Sec. 4: *"Every person shall be at liberty to worship God according to the dictates of his own conscience."*

MINNESOTA (1897/1998)

Preamble: "We, the people of the state of Minnesota, *grateful to God for our civil and religious liberty, and desiring to perpetuate its blessings and secure the same to ourselves and our posterity,* do ordain and establish this Constitution."

MISSISSIPPI (1890)

Preamble: "We, the people of Mississippi in convention assembled, grateful to Almighty God, and involving his blessing on our work, do ordain and establish this Constitution."

ARTICLE 3, Sec. 18. "No religious test as a qualification for office shall be required; and no preference shall be given by law to any religious sect or mode of worship; but the free enjoyment of all religious sentiments and the different modes of worship shall be held sacred. The rights hereby secured shall not be construed to justify acts of licentiousness injurious to morals or dangerous to the peace and safety of the state, *or to exclude the Holy Bible from use in any public school of this state.*"

MISSOURI

Preamble: "We the people of Missouri, *with profound reverence for the Supreme Ruler of the Universe, and grateful for His goodness,* do establish this constitution for the better government of the state."

ARTICLE 1, SEC. 5 *"That all men have a natural and indefeasible right to worship Almighty God according to the dictates of their own consciences."*

MONTANA

Preamble: "We the people of Montana, *grateful to God for the quiet beauty of our state, the grandeur of our mountains, the vastness of our rolling plains, and desiring to improve the quality of life, equality of opportunity and to secure the blessings of liberty for this and future generations* do ordain and establish this constitution."

NEBRASKA

Preamble: "We, the people, *grateful to Almighty God for our freedom,* do ordain and establish the following declaration of rights and frame of government, as the Constitution of the State of Nebraska."

ARTICLE 1. Sec. 4. *"All persons have a natural and indefeasible right to worship Almighty God according to the dictates of their own consciences."*

NEVADA

Preamble: "We the people of the State of Nevada, *Grateful to Almighty God for our freedom in order to secure its blessings,* insure domestic tranquility, and form a more perfect Government, do establish this Constitution."

NEW HAMPSHIRE (1784/1990)

[Art.] 5. [Religious Freedom Recognized] *"Every individual has a natural and unalienable right to worship God* according to the dictates of his own conscience, and reason."

NEW JERSEY (1947)

Preamble: "We, the people of the State of New Jersey, *grateful to Almighty God for the civil and religious liberty which He hath so long permitted us to enjoy, and looking to Him for a blessing upon our endeavors to secure and transmit the same unimpaired to succeeding generations,* do ordain and establish this Constitution."

NEW MEXICO (1911/1974)

Preamble: "We, the people of New Mexico, *grateful to Almighty God for the blessings of liberty, in order to secure the advantages of a state government,* do ordain and establish this Constitution."

NEW YORK (1938/2002)

Preamble: "We, The People of the State of New York, grateful to Almighty God for our Freedom, in order to secure its blessings, do establish this constitution."

NORTH CAROLINA

Preamble: "We, the people of the State of North Carolina, *grateful to Almighty God, the Sovereign Ruler of Nations, for the preservation of the American Union and the existence of our civil, political, and religious liberties, and acknowledging our dependence upon Him for the continuance of those blessings to us and our posterity,* do, for the more certain security thereof and for the better government of this State, ordain and establish this Constitution."

ARTICLE 1. Sec. 13. *"All persons have a natural and inalienable right to worship Almighty God according to the dictates of their own consciences, and no human authority shall, in any case whatever, control or interfere with the rights of conscience."*

NORTH DAKOTA

Preamble: "We, the people of North Dakota, *grateful to Almighty God for the blessings of civil and religious liberty,* do ordain and establish this constitution."

Section 3. *"The free exercise and enjoyment of religious profession and worship, without discrimination or preference shall be forever guaranteed in this state."*

OHIO

Preamble: "We, the people of the State of Ohio, *grateful to Almighty God for our freedom, to secure its blessings and promote our common welfare,* do establish this Constitution."

§ 1.07 "Rights of conscience; education; the necessity of religion and knowledge (1851) *All men have a natural and indefeasible right to worship Almighty God according to the dictates of their own conscience. . . . Religion, morality, and knowledge, however, being essential to good government, it shall be the duty of the general assembly to pass suitable laws to protect every religious denomination in the peaceable enjoyment of its own mode of public worship, and to encourage schools and the means of instruction."*

OKLAHOMA (1907/1975)

ARTICLE I. Sec. 2 *"Perfect toleration of religious sentiment shall be secured, and no inhabitant of the State shall ever be molested in person or property on account of his or her mode of religious worship."*

OREGON (1857/1859)

Article 1, Section 2. *"All men shall be secure in the Natural right, to worship Almighty God according to the dictates of their own consciences."*

PENNSYLVANIA

Preamble: "We, the people of the Commonwealth of Pennsylvania, *grateful to Almighty God for the blessings of civil and religious liberty, and humbly invoking His guidance,* do ordain and establish this Constitution."

ARTICLE I. Sec. 3 *"All men have a natural and indefeasible right to worship Almighty God according to the dictates of their own consciences."*

ARTICLE I. Sec. 4 *"No person who acknowledges the being of a God and a future state of rewards and punishments shall, on account of his religious sentiments, be disqualified to hold any office or place of trust or profit under this Commonwealth."*

RHODE ISLAND (1843)

Preamble: "We, the people of the State of Rhode Island and Providence Plantations, *grateful to Almighty God for the civil and religious liberty which He hath so long permitted us to enjoy, and looking to Him for a blessing upon our endeavors to secure and to transmit the same,* unimpaired, to succeeding generations, do ordain and establish this Constitution of government."

ARTICLE I. Sec. 3 *"Whereas Almighty God hath cerated the mind free;* and all the attempts to influence it by temporal punishments or burdens, or by civil incapacitations, tend to beget habits of hypocrisy and meanness; *and whereas a principal object of our venerable ancestors, in their migration to this country and their settlement of this state, was, as they expressed it, to hold forth a lively experiment that a flourishing civil state may stand and be best maintained with full liberty in religious concernments; . . ."*

SOUTH CAROLINA

Sec. 2. *"The General Assembly shall make no law respecting an establishment of religion or prohibiting the free exercise thereof,* or abridging the freedom of speech or of the press; or the right of the people to peaceably to assemble and petition the government or any department thereof for a redress of grievances."

SOUTH DAKOTA

Preamble: "We, the people of South Dakota, *grateful to Almighty God for our civil and religious liberties . . .* do ordain and establish this Constitution for the State of South Dakota."

ARTICLE 6. Sec. 3. *"The right to worship God according to the dictates of conscience shall never be infringed."*

TENNESSEE

ARTICLE I. Sec. 3 "That *all men have a natural and indefeasible right to worship Almighty God according to the dictates of their own conscience . . .*"

TEXAS

Preamble: *"Humbly invoking the blessings of Almighty God, the people of the State of Texas, do ordain and establish this Constitution."*

UTAH

Preamble: *"Grateful to Almighty God for life and liberty,* we, the people of Utah, in order to secure and perpetuate the principles of free government, do ordain and establish this Constitution."

VERMONT (1793)

Article 3. *"That all persons have a natural and unalienable right, to worship Almighty God, according to the dictates of their own consciences and understandings, as in their opinion shall be regulated by the word of God."*

VIRGINIA

ARTICLE I. Sec. 16. *"That religion or the duty which we owe our Creator, and the manner of discharging it, can be directed only by reason and conviction, not by force or violence; and, therefore, all men are equally entitled to the free exercise of religion, according to the dictates of conscience; and that it is the mutual duty of all to practice Christian forbearance, love, and charity to each other."*

WASHINGTON

Preamble: "We, the people of the State of Washington, *grateful to the Supreme Ruler of the Universe for our liberties,* do ordain this constitution."

WEST VIRGINIA

Preamble: *"Since through Divine Providence we enjoy the blessings of civil, political and religious liberty,* we, the people of West Virginia, in and through the provisions of this Constitution, *reaffirm our faith in and constant reliance upon God* and seek diligently to promote, preserve and perpetuate good government in the state of West Virginia for the common welfare, freedom and security of ourselves and our posterity."

WISCONSIN

Preamble: "*We, the people of Wisconsin, grateful to Almighty God for our freedom, in order to secure its blessings,* form a more perfect government, insure domestic tranquility and promote the general welfare, do establish this constitution."

WYOMING

Preamble: "We, the people of the State of Wyoming, *grateful to God for our civil, political and religious liberties, and desiring to secure them to ourselves and perpetuate them to our posterity,* do ordain this Constitution."

---

[1] Italics for emphasis only

SELECTED
BIBLIOGRAPHY

BOOKS, ARTICLES, DOCUMENTS

American Academy of Pediatrics Committee on Public Education. "Media Violence," *Pediatrics*. Vol. 68, No. 5. November 2001 via http://www.aap.org.

Barclay, William. *The Ten Commandments*. Westminster: John Knox Press, 2003.

Bork, Robert H. *Coercing Virtue: The Worldwide Rule of Judges*. Washington, D.C.: AEI Press, 2003.

Bork, Robert H. *The Tempting of America: The Political Seduction of the Law*. New York: Free Press, 1990.

Briscoe, D. Stuart. *The Ten Commandments: God's Rules for Living*. Colorado Springs, CO: WaterBrook Press, 1995.

Calvin, John. Benjamin W. Farley, trans. *John Calvin's Sermons on the Ten Commandments*. Grand Rapids, MI: Baker Books, 2001.

Carter, Chelsea J. "U.S. Leads Richest Nations in Gun Deaths." *Associated Press*. April 17, 1998 via http://www.guncite.com.

Cheever, George B., ed. *The Journal of the Pilgrims at Plymouth in New England, in 1620* via http://www.churchstatelaw.com.

Conlin, Michelle with Jessi Hempel. "Unmarried America." *Business Week Online*. October 20, 2003 via businessweek.com.

Cromie, William J. "System Tracks Gun Deaths: Details Are Being Collected on Murders, Suicides in the U.S." *Harvard University Gazette*. September 28, 2000 via http://www.news.harvard.edu.

Davidman, Joy. *Smoke on the Mountain: An Interpretation of the Ten Commandments*. Westminster: John Knox Press, 1985.

Devlin, Patrick. *The Enforcement of Morals.* London; New York: Oxford University Press, 1965.

Elliot, Jonathan. *The Debates of the Several State Conventions on the Adoption of the Constitution.* 2d ed. Philadelphia, PA: J. B. Lippincott Company, 1907.

Federer, William J. *The Ten Commandments and Their Influence on American Law.* St. Louis, MO: AmeriSearch, Incorporated, 2002.

Foundation for Individual Rights in Education. "FIRE Survey." November 2003 via http://www.thefire.org.

Hanson, Jeff. *The Mars Hill Review.* No. 12. Bainbridge, WA: Mars Hill Forum, Fall 1998.

Hill, Napolean. *Think and Grow Rich.* Los Angeles, CA: Renaissance Books, 2001.

Hillman, James. *The Force of Character and the Lasting Life.* New York: Random House, 1999.

Himmelfarb, Gertrude. *One Nation, Two Cultures.* New York: Knopf, 1999.

Hybels, Bill. *Engraved on Your Heart: Living the Ten Commandments Day by Day.* Colorado Springs, CO: Cook Communications Ministries, 2000.

Inaugural Addresses of the Presidents of the United States from George Washington to Bill Clinton. Champaign, IL: Project Gutenberg; e-Books.

Isaac, Robert and Samuel Wilberforce, *The Life of William Wilberforce.* Vol. 1. London: John Murray, 1838.

Joseph, Mike M. *Middle East: Blueprint for the Final Solution: The Coming Fall and Rise of Western Democracy.* Bloomington, IN: 1stBooks Library, 2003.

Kimball, Roger. *The Long March.* San Francisco: Encounter Books, 2000.

Kramer, Noah. *Mythologies of the Ancient World.* Anchor, 1960.

Kroft, Steve. "Porn in the U.S.A.." *60 Minutes.* November 21, 2003 via http://cbsnews.com (broadcast November 25, 2003).

Laband, David N. and Deborah Hendry Heinbuch. *Blue Laws: The History, Economics, and Politics of Sunday-Closing Laws.* Lanham, MD: Rowman & Littlefield, 1987.

Lasch, Christopher. *The Revolt of the Elites and the Betrayal of Democracy.* New York, NY: W. W. Norton, 1995.

"Making It Add Up." *Los Angeles Times* editorial. April 21, 1986.

Martin, Glen S. *God's Top Ten List: The Ten Commandments.* Chicago, IL: Moody Press, 1999.

Mehl, Ron. *The Ten-der Commandments: Reflections on the Father's Love.* Sisters, OR: Multnomah Publishers, 2001.

Mikva, Rachel S., ed. *Broken Tablets: Restoring the Ten Commandments and Ourselves.* Woodstock, VT: Jewish Lights Publishing, 1999.

Moore, Thomas. *Care of the Soul.* New York, NY: HarperCollins, 1992.

Morgan, G. Campbell. *The Ten Commandments.* Emerald House, September 1997.

Murray, Andrew. David Hazard, ed. *Mighty Is Your Hand.* Minneapolis, MN: Bethany House Publishers, 1994.

National Commission on Excellence in Education. "A Nation at Risk." April 26, 1983 via http://www.ed.gov.

Neuhaus, Richard John. *The Naked Public Square: Religion and Democracy in America.* Grand Rapids, MI: W. B. Eerdmans, 1984.

Nisbet, Robert. *Prejudices: A Philosophical Dictionary.* Cambridge, MA: Harvard University Press, 1982.

O'Callaghan, E.B., ed. *Documents Relative to the Colonial History of the State of New-York* via http://www.churchstatelaw.com.

Penn, William. *Select Works of William Penn. To Which is Prefixed a Journal of His life* via http://www.churchstatelaw.com.

Peterson, Merrill D., ed. *Thomas Jefferson: Writings* 346–48 (1984) via http://www.churchstatelaw.com.

Phillips, Timothy R. and Dennis L. Okholm, eds. *Christian Apologetics in the Postmodern World.* Downers Grove, IL: InterVarsity Press, 1995.

Poore, Ben Berley, ed. *The Federal and State Constitutions, Colonial Charters, and Other Organic Laws of the United States 1888–93.* 2nd ed. via http://www.churchstatelaw.com.

Rabkin, Jeremy. *Why Sovereignty Matters.* Washington, D.C.: AEI Press, 1998.

Reisman, Judith A. *Kinsey: Crimes & Consequences.* 2nd Edition. Crestwood, KY: The Institute for Media Education, Inc., 1998, 2000.

Rushdie, Salman. *The Satanic Verses.* New York, NY: Picador, 2000.

Salemi, Peter. "The Plain Truth about Islam and Other Religions" via www.cgsf.org.

Schlessinger, Laura and Rabbi Stewart Vogel. *The Ten Commandments: The Significance of God's Law in Everyday Life.,* New York, NY: HarperCollins Publishers, 1998.

Shane, Scott. "Locked Up in Land of the Free." *Baltimore Sun,* June 1, 2003.

Singh, S., & Darroch, J.E. "Adolescent Pregnancy and Childbearing: Levels and Trends in Developed Countries." *Family Planning Perspectives* 32: 2000.

Statistical Abstract of the United States: 2002. 122nd Ed. Washington, D.C.: U.S. Census Bureau.

Stedman, Edmund C. and Ellen Hutchinson eds. *IV A Library of American Literature* 36–38 via http://www.churchstatelaw.com.

Tozer, A. W. *The Knowledge of the Holy.* New York, NY: Harper & Brothers, 1961.

A. W. Tozer, *The Root of the Righteous.* Chicago, IL: Moody Press, 1955.

Van Biema, David. "Buddhism in America." *Time.* October 13, 1997.

Washington, George. "The Farewell Address." *The Papers of George Washington.* University of Virginia via http://gwpapers.virginia.edu.

Washington, Henry A., ed. *8 The Writings of Thomas Jefferson* via http://www.churchstatelaw.com.

Weber, Max. *The Sociology of Religion.* Boston: Beacon Press, 1963.

West, Michael D. "Back to Immortality: The Opportunities and Challenges of Therapeutic Cloning." *Life Extension Magazine.* Fort Lauderdale, FL: Life Extension Media LLC, November 2003.

Wolfe, Alan. *The Transformation of American Religion: How We Actually Live Our Faith.* New York, NY: Simon & Schuster/Free Press, 2003.

WEBSITES

FindLaw via http://www.findlaw.com

FrontPage Magazine, August 23, 2000, via http://www.frontpagemag.com

Hinduism Today, via http://www.hindunet.org

Legal Information Institute via http://www.law.cornell.edu

PBS NewsHour via http://www.pbs.org

The Supreme Court via http://www.supremecourtus.gov

World Jewish Congress via http://www.wjc.org.il